Thinking About Film
A Critical Perspective

Dean Duncan
Brigham Young University

PEARSON

Boston New York San Francisco
Mexico City Montreal Toronto London Madrid Munich Paris
Hong Kong Singapore Tokyo Cape Town Sydney

CONTENTS

Touched on in vols - 8\&9

PREFACE

Statement of Purpose

The aim of this small book is to help its readers become more active, intelligent film viewers. In order to do so we will learn about some of the wide range of stories and stylistic strategies utilized by film artists and film institutions. We will touch upon some of the practical elements of filmmaking (screenwriting, directing, acting, production design, cinematography, editing, music and sound, etc.) that enable filmmakers to tell their stories, and communicate their messages. Just as importantly, and more especially, we will explore some new and helpful ways of receiving films. As we think about how to evaluate and analyze the movies we see, we will learn that the act of viewing (and hearing) can be just as creative, and as satisfying, as activities usually ascribed to filmmakers and other artists.

In order to illustrate this point we will have occasion to go beyond practical production questions, and to think about more than just the commercial films with which many viewers are most familiar. We will also consider the place and importance of film history, of the documentary and international film, of the critical and ethical components of filmmaking and film viewing. These things will challenge us in ways to which we may not be used. Challenge can be invigorating. Attention to these additional contexts can remove the reader, if he or she is willing, from the passive, self-centered demand for mere entertainment and escape that is so characteristic of contemporary film culture.

All of this may require us to shift a bit. There is, of course, nothing wrong with entertainment, and everyone benefits from an escape now and then. But movies can do more for us, and with us. We will be talking a lot about that potential, and how we can help the process along. Some of you already know about the intellectual engagement and invigoration that film can provide. Others of you don't go to movies to be invigorated. Here lies our challenge, and our opportunity.

This book is written for students who are starting their college and university careers, and for anyone who wants to get a little more out of the film viewing experience. With all due respect to those who just want to have fun, it is written with the assumption that intellectual invigoration is desirable, and necessary, and that movies rightly received are capable of providing it. This is true in a number of ways, and for a number of reasons.

For those of you who are starting your college careers, we will look to demonstrate and foster something that will be required of you all, regardless of the course of study you choose. Higher education teaches you to think critically, to see a situation from different angles, to consider different perspectives. Higher education teaches you to use a combination of vigor and sympathy as you synthesize information, and as you reach and act upon conclusions. Critical thinking is not exclusive to higher education. Whether or not you are seeking a university degree, these things are important, and even essential.

In addition to having these aims, thorough education also has its methods. In this introduction you will already have noticed the frequent use of the word "we." This usage is not meant to be precious or mannered, but to suggest something of what can and should happen in an effective educational exchange. There is a teacher and there is a student, and both parties listen to and engage with one another. *Thinking About Film* shares the aims of a dialogue, an ancient literary form that is more than just lecturing and note taking.

Dialogues are designed to stir their participants out of intellectual apathy, to help them to interrogate preconceptions and become more conscious of what they think and do. Dialogues ask provocative questions, and imply that their participants actually seek answers. As such, the questions in a dialogue, and the questions that fill this book, are real ones. They require and reward real attention, and real responding, in the classroom, and beyond.

Dialogues can sometimes be spirited, but they need not be confrontational. They can take place between members of a community, between people who not only differ, but who are committed to one another, who are interested in compromise and reconciliation and inclusive social action. In the end, the aim of this book is not simply to provoke. We will touch upon complicated and even controversial issues, but in a more informal tone than you will usually find in scholarly discourse. This is to imply that we are not in a debate, but a conversation, with all of the sympathy and open-endedness that word suggests.

There are practical consequences and practical dividends that go with the serious study of film. The ideas that movies express and the issues that they reflect can provoke and divide. But the ideas that movies express and the issues that they reflect can also lead us beyond ourselves and into community, even beyond the more self-absorbed aspects of our youth, and into gainful adulthood. Many film institutions treat us like consumers, and much cultural discourse takes the form of mere confrontation. We can be more, and we can do better.

Films, and the Arts in general, can lead us into effectual citizenship, into a political conversation that goes beyond the divisive partisanship of the culture wars. Films, and the Arts in general, can help us figure out what we believe, and how to responsibly act on those beliefs. They lead us to think about principles, and about maintaining them while we respect the principles of others. This isn't just politics; it is civics, or conviction and courtesy brought together, bearing the fruit of ethical impulse and action.

Summary of Sections

This book has a simple structure. One chapter builds upon the next, with the whole hopefully culminating in an expanded set of intellectual insights and critical skills. The first chapter, "Evaluation and Analysis: Some Critical Criteria," identifies some common conventions of popular critical discourse. These familiar conventions are effective in part, and they also have some serious limitations. An alternative is proposed that synthesizes a number of sensibilities into a critical strategy that is simultaneously rigorous and generous. Subsequent chapters illustrate the application of this strategy at the same time that they supplement the terms and tools with which it might be applied.

The second chapter is "Getting Started: The Films You See and the Things You Think." It concerns critical thinking, as well the timely matter of media literacy. Not surprisingly, this section also concerns the actual viewer, and specifically the ways that many of us watch and think about films. Included are two exercises. The first reveals what may be patterns of passivity in the way we make media choices. The second suggests some of the great personal resources we can draw upon as we step up to more rigorous and satisfying analytical activity.

With this greater understanding of ourselves and our mental processes, we proceed to the third chapter. "Standards of Judgment" is a discussion about finding value and substance in film. In this part of the text we will consider not only the films themselves, but the activity of viewing, of thinking, and of integrating all of this into a wider set of issues and communications.

Chapter 4, "Sources and Settings," explores some textual options that may be unfamiliar, the kinds of films that will test and increase our critical mettle, as well as our literacy and enjoyment. Having thought about ourselves, and having considered ways we can more effectively think about and relate to the world, we proceed to fifth chapter. "The Elements" is a discussion of the different crafts that constitute the art and business of film.

The final section of the book summarizes and synthesizes what has gone before, and suggests where we might go from here. We close by briefly considering critical writing, and how we can express and communicate some of the things we have been discussing to others. Useful supplementary material is also provided in a section of appendices.

CHAPTER 1
EVALUATION AND ANALYSIS: SOME CRITICAL CRITERIA

Introductory film classes at the college level tend to touch upon many things. One of the most important of these is the institution and practice of film criticism. There are always a few students that bring some knowledge and experience to that conversation. They have read a number of different critics, or have familiarized themselves with a few of the many film periodicals that devote themselves to the subject. Others have not read as widely. Inevitably a couple of these less experienced students will express what is really quite a common complaint about film and media criticism: they don't like critics because they don't agree with them.

This is an interesting and in many ways understandable sentiment. We disagree with much of what we hear in the culture around us, and this is often as it should be. Our disagreements may stem from valid differences in disposition or sensibility. They may even turn on some key moral point, on a principle that we are not willing to compromise. (With regard to film, our disagreements may also turn on the fact that a lot of contemporary film criticism is really poor, but that is a whole different topic.)

Still, for all of our scruples, and for however much we may think otherwise, it is not always principle that causes us to disagree with or even object to critical discourse. There is a reality that many stubborn students feel to resist, but which is nevertheless, demonstrably and repeatedly, true. When we are resistant to criticism, or to unfamiliar things that are being criticized (analyzed, etc.), precept is not always what motivates us. Sometimes our critical resistance is simply and straightforwardly due to a closed mind, or a lack of intellectual industry.

Having an Open Mind

This is an important issue and it extends beyond our mere experiences with the movies. We often resist people, critics in this case, with whom we disagree. We should think more about this reflex. Should we only talk or listen to those who think like we do? A world made in our own image, which conforms and limits itself to what we know and desire, will surely be a pinched and paltry place. On the other hand, though it is true that opening ourselves to things that we had never contemplated can be a humbling and disconcerting experience, it is also true that an open-hearted participation in the exchange of ideas and observations can lead to much growth and edification.

Our involvement in positive, constructive critical conversations can facilitate just this kind of growth and edification. Such conversations can help us in our own search for interesting and substantial media, as well as for better ways to understand and gain from it. This book is attempting to model just this kind of conversation. As it does so it is important to establish that we are not trying to make definitive judgments, or to have the reader always agree. We will proceed together on the assumption that the open airing of perspectives and possibilities, for all the complications it entails, will ultimately help us understand others, and ourselves, better. To this point the reader may agree; these are not particularly controversial ideas. However it might be said that, as stated, they are too abstract to be of much use. Questions naturally arise: what specifically does one do? How can one take part? This book seeks to answer some of these questions. In this section you will find a few basic critical principles, the consideration and application of which will equip readers for the critical work, and the fun, to follow.

A Work Should Be Judged on Its Own Terms

It is important to know that the way things are usually done is not necessarily the way things should, or must be done. This is extremely true of the movies. Most commercial story telling tends toward closure, a neat and satisfying conclusion that answers all of our story-related questions and solves all of our story-related problems. In addition a great deal of the critical writing that we find, whether the object of criticism is commercial and intends closure or not, reflects this same impulse. There is a reason for this. We are understandably reassured by clear answers to important questions: what does it mean? Is it good or is it bad? Should I spend my time and money on this thing?

But in this approach there is a potential problem. It may be that a consumer report about a product with a very specific purpose can be appropriately and effectively made in the way just described. It is certainly true that the people that make these products benefit from such cut and dried conversation, at least if the consumer report is positive. But as students and teachers, neighbors and citizens, should we be satisfied by mere product ratings?

The fact is that the commercial and critical closure characteristic of the workaday production and discussion of movies is incompatible with the expansive, searching discussion that leads past mere entertainment to education. Much of our cultural expression and many of our social interactions are being dominated by a kind of transaction approach—we buy and sell, and consume, and then rush heedlessly on. There is a time and a place for commerce, but this approach has had an unfortunate, even dangerous effect on the way we think and interact. The reason for this is that it really has little resemblance to what we know, and who we are.

People are complicated, groups of people are even more complicated, and that complexity is inevitably, confoundingly, and wonderfully a part of any expression of individual or community life. It takes time and patience to get to know someone, or something that is an expression or reflection of that person. Products may be straightforwardly this or that, but the books and movies and programs and people that are most worth our while require a little more of us.

If these things are true, then they should affect the way we read and see, and they may require us to make some fundamental changes. Though superficial practices are all around us, we are not obligated to follow suit. Too many critics and spectators reach for definitive judgments without first thinking about the criteria on which something should be judged. We are at risk if we hasten to critical conclusions without giving any time or thought to the conversations that would give them meaning.

If this is the case, then two critical principles should follow. The first of these principles is that a work should be judged on its own terms, and not on the basis of some other prevailing custom or preference or expectation. When we consider a film or program we should try to identify what it is and how it operates. We want to understand the way it is structured, and something of the intent behind it. Rather than imposing upon it, we want to be reasonably open, and attend to it.

This means that a story that seeks to raise questions should not be faulted when it doesn't give answers. A small character-based film is not a failure because it does not resemble a big-budget special effects extravaganza. We need not reject the Iranian feature that moves at a more leisurely pace than the action-adventure picture from Hong Kong. An old movie is not the lesser for not being a new movie.

This does not mean that the thoughtful viewer must endorse every film that does what it wants. Intention is just one consideration among many, and if one feels a film's objective to be questionable, then one should say so. For instance, films that advocate and model materialism or destructive self-absorption, even—especially—if they do so unconsciously, might be considered and then possibly condemned on their own materialistic, self-absorbed terms. But we want to listen to the film first, and not just throw it out because of our deafness or our insensitivity to its language.

The Responsibility for a Good Film Experience Lies with the Viewer

The second critical principle is closely related to the first. Much media product is distributed on the assumption that audiences are demanding and passive and requiring that everything be done for them. A critical, educational consideration of the media runs directly counter to this truism: the fact is that much of the responsibility for a good film experience lies with the viewer. If we are to judge a work on its own merits, according to its own nature, then we must do some thinking, maybe even some studying in order to understand that nature.

Much of the conversation that follows in this book will explore ways through which we can achieve this kind of thoughtful understanding. One of the most important of these methods is not practiced as often as it might be, perhaps because it runs counter to the economically competitive and ideologically divisive nature of much film discourse. It is that, in the sense discussed in this book's preface, we can have a dialogue with a film. We can listen carefully and respond prudently. We can combine criticism with empathy. As we do so, we will find unsuspected rewards.

If a film is falling short the sympathetic viewer need not simply condemn it, or reject it, or run from it. By his simultaneously rigorous and generous attention, he can describe a difficulty, identify a cause, and continue to be entertained or informed. This is possible when one learns about the crafts of filmmaking (further explored in chapter five). It is also possible when we step back from the film itself, or the money we are afraid we wasted on it, to think about context. What social or historical factors might have contributed to this unclear or unacceptable thing? How might this apparent difficulty or inadequacy become a source of deeper critical or historical insight?

In sum, a combination of generosity, curiosity, and a willingness to think things through and work things out will actually bring the viewer into the creative process. This means that the challenges, invigorations and satisfactions of art making need not be restricted to those with the money and the equipment and the means of distribution. These are the things we are looking for, the things we hope to accomplish in our conversations here.

These principles should have some consequence to the reader's experience with this very book. You will encounter firm statements of strong opinion. You may well, indeed should sometimes disagree with those judgments. But our perspective, though it may differ from most consumerist, reductively evaluative criticism, is that this differing is not inherently a problem. Rather than offering definitive conclusions we are interesting in continuing conversations, helping each other to discover and consider angles or nuances that we would not have found on our own. We will proceed on the assumption, and with the conviction, that there are many valid and instructive approaches to any idea or representation. To discuss and consider these alternatives is to increase our critical vocabulary, to increase our ability to effectively understand and apply the ideas that we encounter.

CHAPTER 2
GETTING STARTED: THE FILMS YOU SEE AND THE THOUGHTS YOU THINK

We have now discussed some valid critical principles. They are useful, but to a degree they are also somewhat generalized, or abstract. We need something concrete, some specific ways to apply all this. If these things are true, what do we do now? We have just spoken of being sensitive to the films that we watch, of considering the intents and strategies of their creators. Effective criticism does these things, but that is not all that is to be done. The message, and the messenger that transmits it, are only a part of any communication. The other essential part of the communication equation has to do with reception, and the receiver. Before we can understand movies, we have to understand ourselves, and the ways that we absorb and process the things around us.

Most of our media experiences are recreational. For some, recreational reading is at least implicitly based on an assumption like the one about the film critics we don't agree with (see above). This assumption is that close study, vigorous analysis and critical thinking take all the fun and pleasure out of our reading.

This assumption is not true. It is not true of the texts that will most challenge and reward us, nor is it true of the friendly, accessible works that we most, and most easily enjoy. Resisting careful analysis contradicts the motivations behind, even the very institutions of higher learning. It also inhibits and even debases the casual conversations that we share with our friends.

Why analyze? Why not simply enjoy things, and then leave them? A comparison may provide some perspective.

Most people like to listen to music. Some, motivated by their listening pleasure, go on to try to learn to play an instrument. As they do so they encounter a daunting obstacle, quite early in the process. It's hard! Where there used to be easy listening enjoyment, now there are new and endless varieties of notes and scales and chord progressions, time signatures and tempos, dynamics and fingering. Students find that in this process of learning recreation turns into labor and for a while, for some, the joy just goes out of the thing.

Why bother? An obvious reason, one that most anyone would grant, is that casual listening is insufficient if one is to become a practitioner. Surmounting those obstacles and internalizing those elements is the sacrifice one makes, the price one pays on her way to competence, or excellence. If during the process there seems to be a loss of former, easy pleasure, then there is consolation in the fact that all that effort will someday lead to more profound satisfactions. It's fun to play music, and even more fun to play it well.

These things are true of more than just music. If one wants to learn a language, or a trade, or an art—if, in the present instance, one wants to learn to be a filmmaker, then one has to bear down. Expertise and excellence have many, many components, and the process of acquisition takes years.

Fair enough. Readers might be thinking that they are not interested in becoming musicians, or filmmakers, and that therefore all this does not apply. We just want to enjoy ourselves.

Here is the key, the great point of departure, the potentially empowering thing. You don't have to be a practitioner to benefit from, or need, training. The informed, theoretical, analytical listener enjoys music more than the casual, distracted listener ever can. Knowing about design enhances our experiences with and enjoyment of our living spaces, even if we never actually fashion them ourselves. If, as was suggested in our discussion of critical criteria, film viewing can be creative, and constructive, if sensitive reading can lead to heightened awareness and deepened application, then it behooves the reader to be just as informed as the practitioner.

Sources of Information: Two Exercises

So, let's be informed, and let us do so by turning briefly to our own selves as objects of analysis. Here are two exercises, two inquiries about things that we have probably taken for granted. The situations, and the questions appertaining thereto, are set forth here. The analysis and the application are left for the reader to perform for him or herself.

Exercise One: Picking Movies

Evaluate the criteria that you use to choose the films that you see. What are the things that get you in that theatre, or seated before that screen? There are any number of sources, all at least partly valid, and all with limitations of which we should be aware. Think of some of those sources: friends and family, grapevines and cooler conversations, commercials and trailers, reviews and awards, the reputation of participants or the subject matter that draws and repels us, the fact that nothing else is on or the rest of the screenings are sold out…

There's a reasonably thorough list. What do you make of it? Have you been aware of these things? Each component bears and rewards some further contemplation, and all of these questions are important. Think about the friends that influence your media choices. What are their interests and ambitions? What is important to them? Are they reflective, or thoughtful? What kind of things do they tend to talk about, and what form does that conversation take? Do they consider your preferences, whether general and social, or specifically related to media consumption? Or, do they often try to impose their will upon you? (We might ask the same question of ourselves!) Are your friends hasty in judgment, or do they give room for conversation, and contemplation?

The same sorts of questions apply to your families. What kind of influence do they have on the things that you see, and the way that you see them? Were there too many Disney movies when you were little, or now that you're getting big? Have you given proper thought to how cool a Western can be? Was the culture of your home broad and deep and expansive, or more pinched than you might have liked it to be? Are the things that you're feeling pinched by actually, or at least partly, a manifestation of real principle and scruple?

Are your parents reluctant to let you grow up and make your own choices? Are they being over-protective? In your own anxiety to grow up, or to prove that you have already done so, are you recklessly disregarding justifiable parental caution?

We have other sources that inform and motivate us. These too should be thought through. Have you ever considered that, as cool as a film trailer or commercial can be, they exist solely to separate you from your money? An advertisement may well set forth a product's real virtues, and we may decide that product to be exactly what we want, or need. But we should think about it a little at first, and be at least a bit skeptical. The guy selling the thing shouldn't be the only person we consult about that thing.

How about this: have you ever noticed how some ostensibly critical conversations (reviews of movies and music and other such things) actually resemble product endorsements themselves? Sometimes writers will try to sell you something, or convince you of something. And they'll use the critical object—the film, the CD, the television program—to do so. This isn't necessarily bad, but you want to give it some thought. What might these reviewers be trying to tell you, or sell you? What is the film itself selling, or the institution that distributes it? Is it simply a particular style, or genre, or subject matter? Or is there something more at issue, some philosophy, or lifestyle, or world view?

If you're using reviewers to help you with your entertainment choices, there's another possibility to think about. Film reviews—this is frequently, though not inevitably true in local, small or medium-sized newspapers, or in reviewer generated websites—are often made up of a plot summary, some vaguely articulated or motivated praise/condemnation, and a glib summary that is quite inadequate to the complexity and contradiction of the actual film. Should we attend to these guys? Alternatively, when the reviews are more thorough, do we consider the nature of the review, or the experience and methodology of the reviewer?

As for awards, have you noticed that sometimes they also have a definite commercial or ideological component? Aren't they sometimes part of a selling strategy? The way that film and television industries celebrate themselves has much to do with bottom lines, since the practitioners that give and receive accolades have a great interest in your patronage. And beyond selling, don't those awards and awards show have a lot to say about partisan politics, or national agendas, or a certain take on geopolitical reality? We should attend to and enjoy and be wary of these conversations.

All of these questions, and others that we might add about a number of other categories, come down to the same basic things. They should make us think. What predilections, pressures and thought processes cause you to choose one film and not another? How do those film choices relate to bigger, deeper, more important things? Have you thought about it all? Shouldn't you do so? We might extend this exercise a little further. Having thought about the criteria with which you choose things, select a film that you have recently seen, and evaluate it on the basis of those criteria. Then reflect. Based on your experience with this particular film, how are your criteria working? Do they lead you to the information that you need? Do they consistently provide you with substantial and enjoyable film experiences? Experiments like this should not be undertaken as simple exercises in self-affirmation. We should push ourselves. To some degree, with regard to our media choices, we are all probably lacking in discernment or discipline or courage. We will want to take aim here at our permissiveness or excess of caution, our sloppiness or smugness or slavery to convention. All this boils down to a culminating question: is there a way for me to make better, more careful media choices?

Exercise Two: Genealogy

Analyzing the criteria we use to pick the movies we see is helpful, and not just for the specific information it provides us. As the questions listed above make clear, this inquiry is also a more general exercise in critical thinking, and critical self-analysis. As with much of the intellectual life that we've talked about, as with many of the challenges that scholars specifically, and adults generally encounter, this exercise reminds us how many important things we take for granted, and the kind of change that more careful attention can provide, or demand.

We could be a little more thoughtful or careful in the way we choose our entertainment. We could also be more thoughtful or careful about things that are even more basic and important.

Do you know about genealogy? Genealogy is concerned with lineage, and with questions of origin. It is concerned with where we came from, and at least implicitly with the ways that descent forms and affects us. For the purposes of this exercise, the genealogical project is adapted somewhat. In addition to familial questions, we are concerned with intellectual and aesthetic lineage. Where did your brain come from? From whence your opinions, and preferences? How do you think, and why?

In the same way that we have actual ancestors, so too are there ancestral events and elements that have helped form you, and the way you relate to and see your world. Have you ever thought about this? How did you come to feel and think the way you do? Who were your most influential philosophical forebears? What experiences formed your tastes, and how? What affect have geography, ethnicity, vocation, denomination, class, color or anything else had on your approach to life, to the arts and, if you like, to film specifically? Have you ever actually thought about any of these things?

One might spend a very great deal of time on this, and that profitably. Consider actually doing so. Make some lists, have some conversations, and add some notes about what you remember, what you have felt and thought about these things: favorite authors, athletes, painters, poets, pets, singers, Sunday School teachers, musicians, mascots; most influential grand/parent, brother/sister, boyfriend/girlfriend, birth/death, art/craft, book/film, sport/team, employment/unemployment, interest/obsession, success/failure, reward/punishment, desire/fear. Is there a certain idea that somehow embodies you, or that you wish embodied you? With what event, or person, or character, do you most identify? What are you most proud, or ashamed of?

An obvious next step would be to take this information about yourself and introduce it into your interactions with friends and family and loved ones generally. Where did they come from, intellectually or philosophically speaking? What is most important to them? Have they actually asked themselves or thought about these things? Do we really understand each other?

These are the some of the questions that biographers ask, the things that take them beyond mere chronologies, or the mere recitation of events. These are some of the questions that facilitate analysis, and lead to understanding. In our own lives we should do more than just think about ourselves, or pursue our own interests. We should know ourselves. This is precisely the end of exercises like these: an increased self-knowledge, and probably a desire to forge and strengthen more substantial connections.

CHAPTER 3
STANDARDS OF JUDGMENT

Thus far we have been setting the stage. We have been discussing critical methodologies, or attitudes, and taking stock of our own mental resources. Now it's time to get down to some detailed, specific film study. All film appreciation courses deal with the elements of the medium, the building blocks out of which movies are made. In this case, this conventional approach happens to be effective and helpful; we are about to treat some of the same issues. When we understand the mechanics of film production—script and story, production design, direction and acting, editing, music, sound, etc.—we can begin to break down the vague impressions that we usually take away from films and step up to another level. On that more particular level, we come to recognize excellence and mediocrity, as well as the component parts of both.

However, there is more to this than the good and bad of film craftsmanship. In addition to questions about whether a film is effectively or efficiently made, we should also concern ourselves with what it is saying. Usually movies tell a story. Is there something else going on? Is the film advocating something, or opposing it? Alternatively, is it presenting us with a situation, or a set of situations, and then leaving us to draw our own conclusions? Is the quality of craftsmanship a part, positive or negative, of the things it is saying? How? In sum, what does it all mean, and what should we think, or do about it?

These questions are more important, and more complicated, than we may have suspected. We spoke earlier about how good musicians and good music listeners should share some assumptions, knowledge and experience. The same goes for writers and readers, for filmmakers and film viewers. We should all do, and we will all benefit from, some hard thinking and working.

Here is where we consider our process, and deepen it. Here is where we change a few things. Many of us are too easily dismissive of films, especially when they treat things with which we are unfamiliar, or that have not interested us. On other occasions, we are too accepting, keying so much on the company we're keeping, or on some appealingly provocative mayhem on the screen, that we miss the implications of what we are seeing. We have all been ignorant or distracted or self absorbed. When we are in these states we may not be able to distinguish between what is excellent and what is substandard, between what builds and what harms.

Critical Thinking and Media Literacy

In this section we will discuss some terms and ideas that will help us to see more clearly. If we have already been thoughtful and careful, these things will help us refine our thinking even further. First thing: *critical thinking* is not the same as simple criticism, or the simple ideas we may have about critical processes. *Critical thinking* isn't the same as thumbs up and thumbs down, or giving films a certain number of stars, or a score out of ten. When we think critically we think calmly. We are reflective about our experiences. We gather information from different sources, considering patterns, clarities and inconsistencies, looking for answers while remembering that simple solutions are not always forthcoming. As critical thinkers we prioritize and synthesize the information that we gather. We draw conclusions and act upon them, at the same time keeping our eyes, and our minds, open to further insight and other possibilities.

As a term and as a concept, *media literacy* is ubiquitous these days. We hear of crises and emergencies, about technological proliferation and media glut, and about the declining level and quality of discourse that has resulted. Much of this talk has to do with young people, with the fact that they are both hyper-familiar with media and technology, and hyper-oblivious to their often enervating effects.

What do you young readers think about all that? Are the adults getting it wrong, once again? Can you describe in detail, and calmly rebut their misconceptions? On the other hand, how much time have you spent texting today? Could it be that these arguments and concerns have some validity?

Media literacy has a lot to do with this whole state of affairs, with identifying both problems and solutions, with taking advantage of the great things that media and technology have to offer without being taken advantage of. And for our purposes, we'll subscribe to a much simpler definition. Like literacy generally, "media literacy" has to do with being able to read and write, and with being able to do so consciously and critically. Here we are concerned with media texts, and specifically with films. ("Writing" in this context also relates to the actual production of films, which is very important, and which lies outside the parameters of our discussion.) We want to know how to read well, and write effectively about the things we read, and see.

There are a number of ideas, a number of categories that can help us as we work to think critically and be media literate. Consider the following, and see how they relate to your own experience, or how they might do so.

Terms and Concepts

Entertainment, escape and escapism

We all like movies for the entertainment they provide. We have all gone to a film in order to forget some pressing problem, at least for a little while. This kind of escape can be therapeutic. It can also be a bit dangerous, especially if our occasional withdrawals become habitual. Think of what the suffix "ism" means. An "ism" is a style, or a philosophy, or even an entire world view. It is a set of ideas on which we base our decisions, and with which we construct our lives.

With all this in mind, do we really want to be escapists? Of course there are plenty of mature and responsible people, people who take on and overcome their real life problems, who also like to wind down once in awhile in a movie theatre. Surely there's no real harm in this. Well, probably not. But with the problems and challenges that there are in the world, we might ask whether passive, empty activity is ever appropriate, or at least whether we should be passive and empty quite as often as we are. Also, are we sure that we are the mature and responsible people aforementioned, those who take on and overcome our real life problems?

In his *Poetics* Aristotle observed that people love to see narratives enacted. We derive great pleasure from the imitation of real life situations. However, for Aristotle that pleasure was based in something that many of us have removed from our entertainment, from our pleasure equations. For him the most abiding narrative pleasure is predicated on learning. Our imitations—plays, movies, etc.—must have substance and magnitude. They must teach us.

Well, many of us may find this prescription to be a bit heavy. Can't we just enjoy ourselves? Of course. But inasmuch as we are discussing scholarly process and scholarly mindsets, we should open ourselves to the idea that there is a lot to learn, and that we haven't set ourselves to the task as we might have, and that it would be well for us to start.

(Do you find, readers, that this last section is a bit too pointed, or preachy? Don't be offended. Remember that we are engaged in a critical dialogue, and that calculated provocation is a proper part of this kind of conversation. Simply think about the ideas being set forth. You may not be guilty. Or, you may be somewhat implicated in the behavior being described. Either way, you will derive the greatest benefit by being calm, self-searching, and good humored, and by considering improvements you might possibly make.)

Passivity and action

Let's discuss some problems. Media passivity in this context means that we're lazy and we want everything done, made clear and resolved, tied up for us. There is a lot of media product that is happy to oblige us in these desires. Is it being produced for you? Do you want a challenge, or do you want simply to be served? There can be two consequences that follow upon this latter desire. The first is that if the communication is clear and its conclusion pleases us, then we won't interrogate it any further. That might not be so good. Is it really okay to kill off the bad guy? Is the attainment of wealth, not to mention the spending of it on self, really the greatest good? There are times when we should question more closely than we do.

The second consequence of passivity is that if the communication requires anything of us, any wrestling or thought or change or even action to follow, we are strongly inclined to just quit. Does that sound right? Aristotle said that a character in a play doesn't come into being, doesn't signify or teach us anything until he acts. The play really gets underway when a choice is made; learning and increase come when the character passes through the consequences that follow. For Aristotle the audience was to be a part of that process too, and his idea is still valid. If we want to learn and grow, if we're not mere escapists, then passive withdrawal is not an option. On the other hand, when we are engaged in active reading and viewing, our experiences begin to contribute to our active living.

Narcissism

Here's another concept connected to the passivity just discussed. There is a lot of narcissism in the way we view media. Narcissism means that we are, or at least we see ourselves as being, the centre and purpose of every exchange or interaction. With regard to film this suggests that we want our viewing experiences to flatter us and confirm us in our every position and assumption. It need hardly be added that such assumptions belong to the childish, or to the victims of arrested development. (How many teenagers does it take to screw in a light bulb? Just one: he simply hangs on and the whole world revolves around him.) It's not a coincidence that a lot of commercial film fare plays to these very sensibilities. Have you ever felt to bemoan the limitations of the films they keep putting out? Look in the mirror. They might be made in your image.

Appropriate Media: Maintaining Moral Principle While Sympathetically Considering the Position of the Other Guy...

This part is tricky. Do you belong to a community of faith? Are you committed to and convicted about what has come to be known as "family values" discourse? If you are then you may have had talks in which the good and bad or right and wrong in movies is represented in terms established by the Motion Picture Association of America's rating system. If it's "G," it's okay. If it's "R," it's not. Perhaps you have sensed that things aren't so simple. "And the PG-13's can be worse than the restricted ones..."

Have you been frustrated by the rating system? Do you sense its shortcomings? Some allege that the MPAA is a site and source of moral erosion, even outright deception or corruption. Have you the sense that the seeming instability of the ratings is part of a deeper difficulty? Many people feel that noble, necessary notions of moral consensus or common community standards have eroded terribly, that the situation is nowhere more evident than in the media, and that we are reaping the whirlwind.

If this is true, it may not all be the MPAA's fault. Certainly it has shortcomings, some of which are acknowledged by and even built into the system. The ratings have no legal basis, they reflect no absolute, and they only represent (sort of) one country's take on things. There have been negotiations over ratings, and film producers have often been calculating, even cynical in the way they conduct the conversation. As for the MPAA itself, it has the difficult task of keeping the moving target of public morality in its sights, trying to serve multiple constituencies who will probably never see eye to eye.

The MPAA's decisions can and should be open to question. But its challenges are enormous. Have we thought this through fairly? Think of the critical criteria that were discussed earlier. We criticize the ratings system (and then, ironically, keep using its terms and categories to define movie morality) without considering its fairly clearly stated, clearly delimited aims. We condemn, without looking closely at what is actually happening.

Take a look at the website. After thoroughly doing so you may still find yourself skeptical about the MPAA's project. In light of the present conversation, however, your skepticism should be leavened by actual listening, and seasoned by sympathetic study. If you have been careful, you may have uncovered a grain of truth that underpins every movie classification system in the world.

Ratings-bashers, and people who are simply concerned about the effects of films, often say that if something's not appropriate for our children, it's not appropriate at all, ever. Fair enough, sometimes. But if that argument were carried too far there wouldn't even be any children. We don't drive at ten, or vote at fifteen, because we have an utterly defensible idea that at those ages we're not yet ready for such important and valid things. This is the useful idea that we can take out of what many feel to be useless ratings. You may believe in milk preceding meat, in lines and precepts building on each other, on dews distilling and maturity being attained. If you are open to these things you may have considered that when we become mature, we're ready to think about some things that grown up people should think about and understand.

Note that we're not discussing pornographies here, but realities. Though we properly guard the kiddies up to a certain point, the time comes that they need to learn about things like sickness and sorrow, war and injustice, even, especially, sin and its consequences. Carefully selected films that are responsibly and intelligently watched can enhance this essential education in a very substantial way. The fact of a rating system can actually facilitate this process.

This part is also tricky. Are you not part of a community of faith? Do you think of believers of various stripes as being somehow suspect, or dangerous? Well, there is zealotry all around, and it's hard to deny that in many cases combinations of excessive scruple, and an excessive willingness to impose it on unsuspecting/unwilling others, has done a very great deal of damage. But we should be very careful about making generalizations, especially when they are prejudicial.

Have you ever thought about ratings, beyond figuring out how to get into a movie that you were too young to see? Have you considered the basic concept behind them? At some ages we are not ready for things that it will eventually become important for us to know. Look at yourselves. Are you (as) mature (as you think you are)? Are you really ready for these conversations? How about the next step? It is unfortunate that some people are so willing, even anxious to take offense. There is an opposite danger. The inability to be offended may actually indicate a loss of precious sensitivities, maybe even of some essential, immemorial scruples. Zealotry and sectarianism aside, is this who or what we want to be?

The suggestion here is that if these issues are often factional, both factions should take a moment to think about the perspective of the other side. You are a liberal. Even so—it may be that some films are inappropriate, whether for you individually, or generally. (Many liberals already feel this to be the case.) Adults can and should consider lots of things, but maturity also implies some sense of restraint, some notion of propriety. Could some of those stridently stated conservative complaints occasionally be true?

If they are, then these things follow. It is possible that an accumulation of violent portrayals in the media can eventually leave some spectators desensitized, even leading a few of them to aggressive behavior. When lives are held cheaply in films, there can be any number of practical, even policy consequences in real life.

One does not necessarily have to be self-righteous to object to harsh language. Such language, whether it be profane or merely confrontational, can be punishing, and painful. Its coarsening effect can diminish the quality and complexity of public conversation. It can make civil conversation, and positive public compromise, very difficult.

A diet of sensual imagery may stir us to actions that have serious or even dire consequences. As non-partisan research on pornography has demonstrated, an accumulation of such imagery can have a destabilizing, even a disastrous effect on our real relationships. Objectifying media can lead us to disrespect bodies, and all the things that are seated there, in real life.

Content and Context, Representation and Advocacy

Is this to say, then, that physical and verbal conflict, or sexual subject matter, should be eliminated from the screen? Perhaps, for you, if you've thought it carefully through and come to that conclusion. Or not. It depends on who you are, and who you want to be. Regardless of your answers to those questions, though, there is an attitude that we should change. Us and them is not as easy and clear cut as we may have thought; as with all of our conversations, whatever the perspective, the idea is that we should consider things more than we have done.

As we grapple with these issues of appropriateness, the notions of content and context, of representation and advocacy can help us. There are helpful, mature films, and there are unhelpful, even exploitative ones. There is also mature viewing, and there is viewing that is less so. Regardless of ideology or allegiance, we should think about ways to distinguish between these binaries. One way to do so is through the following essential concept, one that does a great deal to activate and enable the previously passive viewer.

In a story, appropriateness is not always found in the content as much as in the context in which that content is placed. In other words it is not the subject matter as much as what you (artists and readers!) do with that subject matter that helps or harms. (Context, by the way, is something that the MPAA ratings are not really qualified to address, which is why *The Pianist* and *Old School* get the same rating.)

Consider some examples. We might all agree that in real life murder is unconscionable, and that adultery destabilizes unto destruction. And yet there are many texts—*Macbeth, Crime and Punishment, Night*, Genesis 4: 1-16; *The Scarlet Letter, Madame Bovary, Anna Karenina*, John 8: 1-11—which deal explicitly with these illicit matters, and which do so to our great instruction and edification. This is especially important for those who are concerned about the corrupting influence of media. Representing an objectionable act or idea does not necessarily constitute the advocacy of same. Neither does representation require that we advocate or practice said act, and it does not follow that we will do so. A negative example can teach a positive lesson. And when that negative example is rendered with a simultaneous sympathy for the erring participant, or the things that have driven him to this pass, then our resolve to act ethically is also increased. Principle is affirmed, and sanctimoniousness is avoided.

Irony

Here's another idea that pertains to representation and advocacy, and which may help us to see the many constructive messages that lie embedded in a seemingly cynical culture. We're discussing irony, a rather intractable device that many people find to be troubling. But contrary to rumor, irony is not simply a more sophisticated form of sarcasm. Irony is currently decried by many, but the fact is that there is much use for and much to be gained from a safe and balanced dose of the stuff.

With irony there is a disjunction between the apparent meaning of a statement and its actual, intended meaning. Ironic expressions call attention to incongruities in our lives, to the gap between the ideals that we proclaim and to which we aspire, and the reality for which we too often settle. In emphasizing this discrepancy it may seem that the ironist is placing disproportionate emphasis on negative things at the same time that he or she gives short shrift to, even despairs of the positive. And actually, this is often the case. But if we can remember that the ironist is, more often than not, a disappointed moralist, then we can easily find our way through the disappointment to a clear identification and affirmation of positives.

Theme

We have been moving through partisan waters here, but now we pass on to something thoroughly uncontroversial. We might have begun our discussion of standards of judgment with this topic. We didn't do so because we have been replicating a pattern often encountered in real life. Have you ever found run into hot button issues and held heated conversations over them? Sometimes it is not until much later that we take the time to step back and reflect. Sometimes that time for reflection never comes.

The idea of being open and sympathetic is good, but it has its complications. With all of this bi-partisan back and forth, how do we decide where we stand, who we are, and what we should do? Lurking beneath all of these discussions is the conviction that the arts can help in this, that story not only entertains, but instructs, and expands. One of the most basic and easy ways that it does so is through theme. Of course theme is extremely familiar to all of us, to the point that we may even have forgotten or abandoned it. This is unfortunate, since this easy thing remains central, and essential.

Theme is an elementary-school concept. Almost everyone has learned about themes, and how they work in stories. A theme is a main idea, a message or a statement that comes from a story. Themes can be explicit (obvious). They can be embedded more subtly, or insidiously, within the fabric of the narrative. Every story has one, or as is more likely, several. These may be complementary and consistent, or there may sometimes be contradiction or confusion in their expression. Themes are there whether or not the artist intends them or the reader apprehends them. The artist mostly lies outside our jurisdiction, but when it comes to apprehending, to our own engagement and understanding, we have a part to play in the whole process. When we look for meaning, and even make it on those occasions when the pieces presented to us don't quite cohere, we are going a long way toward having constructive, educational media experiences.

CHAPTER 4
SOURCES AND SETTINGS

We have discussed analysis and criticism, their use and place, and some strategies that can help us positively participate. We have thought about the way we choose our movies, and more importantly, the ways our minds work before and during and after we do so. We have just reviewed a number of critical thinking and media literacy concepts, relating both to the evaluation of media texts and their application to broader contexts.

Most viewers and listeners consume a very small portion of the available, interesting media there is in the world. The multiplex and the usual networks are fine and fun, but they don't always provide the challenge, or allow for the education and expansion that we're looking for. The critical concepts we have just covered equip us for more invigorating intellectual work. In order to do that work, we need some more invigorating settings and sources. Everyone is interested in their own times and places, as they should be. For the moment, however, we seek a wider range.

As discussed, some young film students are resistant to film criticism. A vocal few are even more averse to old movies (especially silent ones), documentaries, and international films. This is unfortunate, in part because everyone should have an interest in past and real and other things. In addition, these possibly unfamiliar sources can be good for us. They almost inevitably force us out of some of our more passive patterns of media consumption. At first we may be challenged, even sorely so. We should make the effort anyway. Here are some reasons.

History and Film

Some people have a notion that history is musty and dusty, long ago and far away, and finally not very relevant to right now. The progressivist myth—that things just keep getting better and better—combines with the fashion conscious person's preference for this year's model and makes some disinclined toward anything old. These feelings are perhaps understandable, since fashions not only come and go, but they can cease to signify. In other words, history presents puzzles that cannot always be solved and questions that don't always have clear answers.

But if our hesitation in the face of the historical has its explanations, it also, ultimately, has no justification either. Why? Present forms come from past practice, and we don't understand the former without considering the latter. On a more personal and maybe more important level, historical awareness does more than help us understand the past. It helps us to sympathize and connect with it, and with the people who inhabited it. For good and ill, we are, individually and collectively, products of what has gone before. As we look sympathetically at the challenges that our forbears experienced, and through which with varying degrees of success they passed, we may find ourselves being a little less hasty, a little less unfairly critical in our contemporary conversations.

Finally there is a less ideological, more immediate benefit of attending to the past. This benefit becomes very clear, and very accessible with regard to the humanities in general, and film specifically. Having made our minor adjustments and found our bearings, the study of history is endlessly interesting, and endlessly enjoyable.

Making History

Though trivia fans and Jeopardy players may disagree, history is not merely a collection of names and dates. Were we to gather all the facts in the world we would still have only the raw material of history, an archive of unorganized matter that couldn't give us any kind of coherent, comprehensible account of the things that happen and what they mean to us. History begins to take shape when a historian starts to sift all that information (including the interpretations of the historians that have gone before), weighing and selecting and ordering the events and the various factors that seem to lead to and follow from them.

It all sounds pretty subjective, doesn't it? Well, so it is, but such subjectivity doesn't invalidate the discipline or practice of history. Events and the people who participate in them are complicated, and it is only in considering perspectives that we begin to get the big picture. Can you really understand the American Revolution without acknowledging the Loyalist cause? Was Neville Chamberlain subject to pressures and even public preference that we no longer recognize? Can we start to comprehend, let alone solve problems between Islam and the West without acknowledging Islam's vast, daunting heterogeneity? Pat, single conclusions are not much more helpful than infinities of uninflected fact. Few of us will be working historians, but as products of and contributors to the endless march of history, it behooves us to gather and compare and interpret historical data just like the professionals do.

A combining of perspectives to get the big picture is especially important in the study of film history. This is because the film industry, like the other entertainment industries, has always been fairly active in obscuring itself, making mythology while it masks its real workings and their real meanings. This isn't (always) a conspiracy, by the way, but careful reading will reveal that a lot of what passes for criticism is really just studio star-making, which the ostensibly objective media too often buys into. Despite a ton of vigorous scholarship over the past many decades, it is still true that much film writing, at least that which is disseminated to lay readers, is bogus: tired anecdotes, received wisdom, show-biz public relations, attempts to steal your money. Film culture has roots and branches and implications that the up-close-and-personal gossip of the newsstand rags can't begin to address.

What is Film History the History of?

So if the stories off the wire services and in the women's magazines don't constitute real film history, where is one to go for the real thing? Well, for one thing, we go beyond the apparent boundaries of the discipline. A lot of the good film scholarship has focused on aesthetic issues, and most of these issues predate the invention of the motion picture camera. Film is literally a culmination and incorporation of most every kind of artistic activity, and its history should also contain the history of all of the arts. When you study literature, or painting and sculpture, or music, or theatre, or design and architecture, you are studying things that pertain very directly to the movies. Not only that, but these disciplines deepen and expand your appreciation of films, and allow you to place them within the great traditions and contradictions of art and communication through human history.

Now the aesthetic elements make for a good start, but art alone is not enough. Film is a business; its study is not complete without considering economic forces, motivations, and realities. Film is technological, and its technological innovations (most of which are responses to or creators of market [economic] pressures) have a profound bearing on aesthetic expression. (As an example, think of changes incident to the coming of sound, color, digital and computer graphics, etc.). Finally, maybe most importantly, those inventions, those economic pressures, those artistic expressions all emerge from and go back into certain social contexts, into art and business and industry, into sociology, psychology, anthropology, ethnography, philosophy, nationality, and on until the end. In other words film, which we can and should enjoy for fun, should also take us back into the real world of real interactions and negotiations, real seekings and real findings. The daunting and exciting fact is that film history is, more or less, the history of everything.

Nostalgia and Genealogy

We have seen how many people are a bit suspicious about history. This can be a problem in an age that is supposed to reflect the final victory of capitalism: there's a lot of old stuff that could bring a profit if properly packaged. One of the ways that cultural industries get around the problem is by evoking and selling nostalgia. They talk about the good old days, the classic tunes, the movies that they don't make like they used to. It's a seductive strategy; many embattled moderns are drawn to this admittedly appealing course because it fosters the illusion, and perhaps partly the reality, that the old days were more innocent, more wholesome, more safe. Nostalgia appears to remove us, if only briefly, from the noxious and complicating realities of today. But isn't this just more Hollywood moonshine?

Nostalgia takes the products and expressions of the past and rips them almost utterly out of context—no aesthetic, economic, technological or social determinants need be acknowledged—presenting them as untroubled, uncomplicated (uninteresting) commodities. The result is that we are alienated from our present because of a false view of our past. It's true that some of life's complications are no fun, but by diluting and defanging history, we may deprive ourselves of its greatest benefits. When it was invented, many observers felt that the great miracle of film was that it could perfectly preserve a permanent record of times, places, relations, faces. That miracle continues to work, at least when we look hard. Fashions and superficial details may pass, but the careful consideration of old films (letters, journals, photographs, etc.) brings us an understanding of the past, which includes its complexity and therefore similarity to our own times, and to our own lives. From such knowledge comes sympathy and fellow feeling.

The Willing Suspension of Disbelief

Samuel Taylor Coleridge's phrase contains an idea that is fairly easy to summarize, and seemingly fairly difficult to apply. Suspending your disbelief does not mean giving up your freedom or individuality, and it does not mean being gullible and accepting anything that they try to put over on you. The willing suspension of disbelief simply means that you give a narrative the benefit of the doubt, that you wish it well and show a willingness to let it into your own life, to work on its own terms, for your profit and enjoyment. It applies not only to narratives that take place on invented worlds—you suspend your disbelief in alien life forms in order to enjoy a certain kind of science fiction story—but also to styles and subject matters that are not contemporary to our own lives. You accept ornamental and digressive writing (Cervantes, or Dickens, or Melville), or the apparent idea that for a woman marriage is the sum and end of all aspiration (Jane Austen), or even a black and white image.

Suspension of disbelief requires that we resist the urge to be self-centered, to see everything on our own terms. It requires not only that our imaginations, but also that our hearts become engaged and open. All of this does not imply the suspension of the critical or the moral sense; we should always be mindful of inconsistent and wary of unseemly elements in our stories. But it does imply that we will be humble enough to let something that we haven't invented or originated or known about already into our lives. No matter what our background or experience, none of us are broad or experienced or sympathetic enough to be able to refuse this challenging and edifying opportunity.

Realism and Formalism

There is a kind of art that places a supreme value on verisimilitude, which is to say that the art piece is supposed to bear a marked resemblance to the actual object or experience being represented. We might call this realism, a multifarious and dangerous term which still gives you an idea of what we're trying to get at. Most people seem to prefer realistic art. In fact, many people seem to think it's the only option. But there is another alternative that is perfectly valid and viable, a fact that we can appreciate when we learn about this alternative and then allow it to work on its own terms.

Formalist art calls attention to the way that something is being said, to the tools and components of the expression, as much as to the statement itself. Verisimilitude is not the goal of formalist art, which is by definition at least somewhat stylized or, if you will, unrealistic. We're consulting Aristotle again: he said that art wasn't art until the creative materials (stone, paint, words, celluloid, etc.) were transformed by the artist. Through that transformation the everyday materials, as well as the object or event—the content—to which they refer, become strange, unfamiliar, artificial. They take us away from what we already know and what we've already experienced, the hope and possibility being that with the transformation of materials and defamiliarization of objects, our very perceptions and feelings will be also changed. Don't get the wrong idea—realism can be glorious. But we need the other approach too, if only because a good formalist experience allows us to return to our realities with new eyes and new sensitivities.

Silent Stylization

This section implicitly endorses not only older films, but also what for most people is the undiscovered country of silent cinema. Few bother with it nowadays. They should. An analogy: Latin, an ostensibly dead language, continues to inform and define a whole family of modern languages. Even a rudimentary knowledge of Latin origins transfigures our experience of and facility with the languages that followed. In a similar way the apparently defunct conventions of silent film lie at the root of modern movie practices. Our attending to the sources illuminates much, most of what follows.

And the appeal is not merely etymological: much of cinema's aesthetic richness, its social substance, its defining economic practices and technological strategies come from the silent period. The silent cinema is very often very beautiful; a disproportionate number of film's most shimmering moments are the direct result of the period's practices and conventions, or can be found in the period itself.

The reason that formalism is so pertinent in a discussion of silent film is that even when its narratives are familiar and its enactments more or less naturalistic, silent film is always stylized. For most people, sound and speech are central components of their lived experience. Silence isn't natural, so its utilization in artistic expression can never be fully realistic. If this is the challenge, then it is also the glory of the silent film.

Lacking access to effective sound technology, early cinema inevitably moved away from realism to the realms of creation and transformation. Silent film was derived from pantomime and partook of the dance, both forms which are generally defined by and enjoyed in the ways that they depart from raw reality. Whether through instinct or by conscious theoretical application, effective artists have always concerned themselves with the characteristics inherent in and unique to their medium. In the early period of film history, silence was one of these elements, and many fine artists exploited it, intentionally and imaginatively. In fact, artificiality was often the centre of a whole strategy of formalized, stylized, transformative filmmaking activity in the silent period.

Again, lots of contemporary people reject silent film (that is if they ever get around to thinking about it) out of plain unfamiliarity or ignorance. They apply one of the philistine's three favorite adjectives: it's weird! ("boring" and "depressing" being the other catch-all dismissals). Well, so is opera, the family, sports, parliamentary democracy, religion, and a whole lot of other things, until you take a little step forward, identify and cease to be alarmed about their stylized characteristics, and simply relax and enjoy.

Documentary

The documentary film has a reputation for sobriety, solemnity, and seriousness of purpose. It concerns itself with causes, crises, and frequently, calls for reform. As a result of these perceptions, all of which coincide with some aspect of documentary reality, many people avoid these films and programs like the plague. Too bad! The fact is that, though they may sometimes be weighty, documentaries also tend to feature interesting characters telling, or living interesting stories, just as in the fiction films we're used to. Non-fiction films contain emotion, humor, conflicts and even reconciliations that are as engaging as any you can find at the multiplex. If it's true that these stories relate more directly to actual lives and our responsibilities as we try to live them more responsibly and substantially, then this should only make them more exciting. They provide an entertainment predicated on learning, even ending in improvement. With docs, you both have and eat the cake at hand. What more can one ask? If you don't like documentary, you haven't tried hard enough.

Three documentary objectives:

1. Exalting the Everyday There are many valid ways to discuss the documentary idiom. They are not and need not be exclusive. That is to say that the following is not necessarily comprehensive or definitive. But it works.

Documentaries seek, whether consciously or not, to validate and value everyday people in their everyday experiences. This flies in the face of most escapist fare, which sees to remove us from the everyday and which, by seeking so to do, indirectly denigrates our ordinariness. Now we know that people have frustrations and difficulties; can't such removal be helpful? Think of a typical fictional scenario. "One day, while Sarah was going to work, she met a tall, dark and handsome man/she was picked up by an alien/she was kidnapped by terrorists..." The point, repeatedly, is that something extraordinary happens, and that the extraordinariness is precisely where our fictional interests and desires lie.

Acknowledging that there is nothing wrong with adventure per say, and that in moderation it has all sorts of benefits, it is also true, and significant, that documentary generally opposes such escapist ideas. Grown-ups don't try, don't need to try to escape all the time. Not only does the everyday have challenges to which we need to attend, it also has satisfactions that can be missed if we overstep the mark. Here's a possible non-fiction scenario. "One day Sarah worked at home, came and went, thought and felt, associated with friends and family, retired, and then got up again the next day to do it again." Isn't that more challenging, more potentially sorrowful or beautiful, than any outlandish scenario that you find at the mall?

2. *A Voice to the Voiceless*   The second objective of the documentary film is to give a voice to the people who don't usually get much of a say in things, and to get power to those who generally have little access thereto. This is very important, even if you happen to have ample representation and power already. After all, effective democracy is partly manifest in the way that the majority that rules treats the minority that doesn't. If, as they say, history is written by the winners, it's not necessarily because that's just and equal and the way it should be.

Ptolemy, and the whole world after him, thought that the earth was the centre of all creation. Little kids feel similarly; watch a toddler walking down the middle of a hallway. He can't conceive of the possibility that anyone might need to get around him, might be going in a different direction. In this there is nothing dishonorable. One acts according to one's lights, and doesn't deserve condemnation for what he or she doesn't know or can't do. Still, Ptolemy and toddlers have a distorted view of the universe and their place in it. Surely growing up means that you start to think a little bit about the other guy, listen to him and then maybe shift your own position as a result. We can't be a part of a community until we start listening to other voices.

Of course there are perils along the way. Communities are not always made up of same thinking, same acting, same voting and believing, even same colored or language'd people. The implications of all this may be inconvenient and difficult, but again, through just this kind of discussion and debate do we get democracy, not to mention great documentary films.

3. *Difficulty and Refinement*   Documentary film deals more consistently than commercial fiction films (at least of the blockbuster variety) with life's real challenges, and they can show us much about how to turn those challenges to our good. We all know this: things are tough, and we won't always succeed, but at least we'd better try to do something about it all. Just as or even more importantly, we'd better not leave other people's difficulties out of the equation, as our own comfort may become pretty threadbare in the face of others' misery. Most of the great religious and ethical traditions hold that this combination of self and other-help is what constitutes a successful, satisfying life. The documentary tradition also holds these things to be self-evident.

Successful, conventional linear narratives often end in satisfying closure, with conflicts settled and problems solved. Documentaries will not do this very often, and for obvious reasons. Our individual challenges, and the difficulties that arise among individuals in communities, are not so easily dispensed with. This may be, and it often is cause for discouragement. Still, there is something to be gained by recognizing and dealing with this fact. Instead of escape or fantasy, we choose reality. We help ourselves, and others, even if we only do so with partial success. And, as happens after a challenging documentary that deals with intractable realities, we are invigorated, increased, and even empowered by the process.

Process and Duration

Documentaries are really good at portraying the processes of labor. Their frequent emphasis on what may seem an undramatic subject actually expresses one of the most basic of documentary principles, which is that work is fundamentally important, and that the worker is worthy of his or her hire. Documentaries also show, perforce, that these processes and labors are long term, not conflicts to solve (a plot point to tie up), but the realities of our lives. We have to work, for all we may wish, or try, to avoid the fact.

The non-fiction film's frequent emphasis on process and duration, on the things we do and the amount of time it takes us to do them, lead us to an essential reality. Most of our deepest successes and satisfactions come as a result of these things that we have to do, over and over and over again. That's where personal accomplishment, successful relationships, legislative advance, and social justice come from.

In another connection, if you know anything about craftsmanship or artisanry, you'll know that when skill attends our useful labor, then beauty is the bi-product. This idea pertains to, can illuminate the making of furniture, fabrics or films. It can also be that charitable regard informs labors like these. When they do so, all sorts of exaltations follow. Films, or a film form that attends to these issues, can set a daunting challenge. Documentaries deal with work, and sometimes we have to work as when we watch them, and it is often true that beauty and love are the byproducts of the process.

Ideology

All of the foregoing is very idealistic, and sincerely so. But there are complications to consider. For instance: ideology is the value system, or set of value systems by which we live, the things we take to be true. We are accustomed to thinking we are governed by true and unassailable principles, and this may in part be the case. But we must acknowledge that value systems are man-inflected when they're not man-made, and as has been increasingly pointed out since the days of Marx and Freud and Charles Peirce, the man-made parts serve, in turn, to make us.

Ideology relates to the idea of theme, which we have already discussed. It too carries a story's message or meaning, with the only difference being that ideological messages are even more likely than thematic ones to be accidental or subconscious. The documentary also has a subconscious, but it is fair to say that it often, even usually tries to deal with the ideological implications of the things we take for

26

granted. Documentary films, and the ideologically informed viewing of fictions films, say that we need to understand not only the surface, but the substance of things.

Intention and Reception

As with themes, ideological messages can be explicit or latent, calculated or completely unintentional. Artists (like everybody else) are always saying more or less than they intended, doing better or worse than they meant to. When we understand that this is the case, we can stop assigning all credit and blame—in other words, all authority—to the filmmaker, who after all is only human. We can remember that to a certain degree virtue and malice co-exist in all of us. When appropriate, we can take an erring artist's incomplete, unfocused, even negative expression and make it a positive reading or viewing experience through our own thought and reflection and application. Furthermore, we can open ourselves up to the very real, insufficiently considered possibility that we might be the ones thinking incompletely, without sufficient focus or rigor, negatively. Either way, vigilance and sympathy, combined in appropriate measure, can transform error, unwitting and even advocated, into our advantage and increase.

Representation and Advocacy, II

These terms were already discussed above, in the "Standards of judgment" chapter. That discussion touched upon the usual hot button items, on screen violence, and sexuality, and harsh language. It was suggested that sometimes you can mention negative things without advocating them, with potentially positive results. Here in our documentary section we will find that representations, and advocacies besides, are very different from the things that we generally key upon in our media discussions.

We have touched upon the differing perspectives that people with different faiths, both sectarian and secular, can have. This setting is relevant to the present subject. The stories and messages that we find in non-fiction films are frequently social and political. They are transmitted in the context of debate and general cultural discourse. In this context the righteousness/wickedness axis that properly and complicatedly informs so many lives shifts uncomfortably, and wonderfully.

Let's be blunt here. We all have our notions of what is true, and sometimes what we take to be true is more informed by ideology, is more transitory than we might like to admit. Further, there is doctrine, and then there is social practice mistaken for doctrine. Documentary culture—which can be said to look back to Marx and the New Testament for its main inspirations—can disturb some of these deep assumptions. It repeatedly speaks for things in which some of you believe deeply (justice, mercy, equality) in ways that leave some of you plain horrified (subsidy, social democracy, even socialism). In fact, without subsidy, social democracy, even socialism, many to most of the landmarks of documentary film would never even have been produced. Neither would some of the undeniable positive change which documentary activism has engendered have occurred. Now what do you say to that?

Some readers will find in that last paragraph an excessive sympathy for what they just know is the ideological dark side. Good—this is an area that promises, to the point of demanding, discussion and debate. Theology of one kind or another, and partisan ideology, dominate many of our lives. The documentary concepts that we have been considering may appear to stand in clear opposition to deepest theological and ideological conviction. The documentary concepts that we have been considering are also fundamentally democratic. Come, let us reason together.

Propaganda

Propaganda is bad, right? Well... It's true that the Nazis and the Stalinists and the advertisers have used it repeatedly, bludgeoningly, for the express purpose of deceiving and threatening and taking your freedom away from you. It's also true that Hollywood, the political candidate you voted for last time and your favorite charity are involved full time in the production of propaganda. The word may be frightening, but the reality is that propaganda means simply the propagating, the sending forth of an idea or a philosophy that one believes in, or at least that one wants others to believe in. If you like, it's a way of bearing a testimony, something that is obviously central to both free religious and political expression.

Clearly a propaganda message can be good, or it can be bad. But as we've already seen, good and bad lies not only in the thing being said, but in the way we're saying it. Watch for this. There is a type of propaganda that's all flying flags and stirring music, distortion and part truths. It might be argued that even a valid message or a seemingly moral/ethical idea is compromised when it is delivered through such means. Those means suggest a lack of confidence in the power of the message, or in the likelihood that the viewer will understand or, more importantly, accept it.

Conversely, as an alternative to this rah-rah method, there is a more reasonable, courteous register of propagandistic communication. In this kind of communication, everything is clear and open, and one is encouraged to hear and think and decide. Once again, we are not talking about pornography here; it may be that in political and social settings, in the so-called marketplace of ideas, this is the more respectful, ethical way, even if it's not your party that's using it. By the way, is documentary propagandistic? Very often. Here is yet another selling point for the media's most important form.

Profit and Merit

Commercial film industries exist for profit, and their definition of profit is usually quite restrictive. We should all be at least a little suspicious of this black ink perspective. Consider the following facts. Many of the milestones of film (and art) history were flops when released. Many of the world's great people were deemed failures, sometimes repeatedly, throughout their lives. Strait is the gate and narrow the way and few there be that find it. Etcetera. Although much of the movie business may work on a contrary assumption, it has been amply and repeatedly demonstrated that there is no necessary correspondence between popularity and merit, or vice versa.

As might be expected, documentaries are built on this paradox. Revenue is part of the picture in non-fiction film, but there are also deeper and more expansive issues that are not tied exclusively to the ledger. Documentarians have often been motivated by sense of social profit or the common good, difficult and essential notions that lead inevitably to abstractions and vagaries that we probably wouldn't want to do without. Did a film on juvenile delinquency help keep an at-risk youth from harm, even though he only saw it at school and so didn't really pay for it at the box office? In calculating what such an exchange might be worth we can add up the cost to the taxpayer of a year in detention, and we can't begin to value the worth of that young man's more constructive, more joyful choices. As with most service and citizenship situations, we take these realities to be incalculable, and undeniable.

International Cinema

Xenophobia: fear of the other. We are comfortable with what is familiar. What is unfamiliar can make us anxious. This natural state of affairs causes many of us to forego wonderful opportunities for growth and enjoyment. As with our historical experiences, our first contacts with other cultures are almost inevitably disconcerting. But if it takes some adjustment and openness to allow for different ways of doing things, then the view that opens up after that adjustment can be extraordinarily exhilarating. While it is humbling to know that our way is not the way, and that the universe does not revolve around us, that humility soon leads to liberation, and even compassion. In the face of such potential gains, the subtitles and unfamiliar conventions of the so-called foreign film are actually minuscule obstacles. An international movie is like another person, another group of people speaking to you from another place. It's better than a t-shirt, and cheaper than a plane ticket— nerves notwithstanding, isn't it better to leave our comfort zones and join the rest of the world?

Foreign and International

What does the word "foreign" suggest to you? Foreign bodies? A foreign object in the ring? The connotations are often quite negative and the word itself is part of the problem, adding just a little bit to the xenophobic temptations that can beset us. This is not mere semantic nitpicking, by the way, nor is it only an incidental point. This issue has universal consequence.

Are any of you foreigners? If that word only suggests a person living in a country that is not her own, then perhaps few would answer in the affirmative. But think harder. Did you ever change schools? Did you not quite fit into, or want to fit into a quarterback and cheerleader culture? Are you a full-bodied woman in what seems like a skinny-bodied world? Are you befuddled by your parents, or by your family culture? Do you like country music? Do you ride a skateboard?

The fact is that there are many things around us that are strange to us, and we may seem pretty strange to a lot of other people. We might apply (or invert) the Golden Rule here. Do we want to misunderstand and reject, as others have misunderstood and rejected us? Instead of being knee-jerkedly phobic about otherness, we might consider the possibility of multiple centers, of the numerous ways there are to get things done. With regard to the present discussion, instead of avoiding foreign films we might start seeking out a few international ones. The prefix "inter" and the word "national" encourage and allow for more connection, for exclusivity to give way to a more inclusive, open mindset. When we let go of our fierce territoriality, we may find that there are more and more places where we feel at home.

Art Film

International films have the reputation of being opaque, artsy, elusive, elitist. Let's get this matter out of the way—they very often are. There are many factors contributing to the situation. And although befuddled beginners may disagree, the emperor being naked is not usually one of them. Many nations have developed remarkably advanced film cultures, which is to say that critics and admission-paying filmgoers are impassioned and informed and demanding. Their film industries, and its workers, respond by producing passionate and demanding work. Thus, the art film.

Unfortunately, paradoxically, since the rise of video the theatrical distribution of international films in North America has dropped to a bare trickle. There was a time, though, from perhaps 1945 (*Rome, Open City*) or 1950 (*Rashomon*) until 1982 (the death of Fassbinder), when these international art films were so successful and so influential as to practically eliminate the notion of borders in film culture, at least for those with eyes to see. One of the reasons for this prospering is that the films stood in extremely marked contrast to the usually timid commercial fare that the studios so often served up. They were different because they were pointed, they were individualized, they were unpredictable, and sometimes they were difficult. You should see them. The task may at first seem daunting, but with a little perseverance you'll find that there are rules operating that can be learned and understood, that there are substantial links to the things that you know and do, and that a new and more substantial entertainment has found its way into your movie lives.

There will, of course, be challenges. An anecdote, or a point of reference: Noel Burch, an American film scholar living in France, was very interested in Japanese cinema, and Japanese culture generally. He did a great deal of watching and reading and thinking, which eventually resulted in an excellent book on Japanese film called *To the Distant Observer* (1979). At the beginning of his book, Burch acknowledged an important lack, suggesting that it had affected his own work, and that it might bear on the reader's own experience with it. This was that, notwithstanding all of his interest and scholarly rigor and hard work, he had not spent a great deal of time in Japan, had only a rudimentary understanding of the language, and did not read it at all. As such, though his interest was great and his observation keen, in the end there remained a great distance.

In saying this Burch was making a proper, honest disclosure. He was also articulating something deeper, something that borders on the universal. We only know so much. When it comes to most people, most places, most things, we are ignorant. We remain on the outside. If we are observant and sympathetic, we become aware of the fact. Our interests and sympathies are aroused, and we start to make connections. Still, we only have so much time, so many resources, and even so much inclination. In most things, even after our best efforts, we remain distant observers.

International films can be elusive even when they're not, so to speak, difficult. The simplest narrative can elude us if we are strangers to the cultural codes that inform them. We may be tempted to turn away. Once again, we should not do so. Here is a situation in which the all-or-nothing, win-or-lose mentality that we so often use may not be appropriate. The fact is that when it comes to cultural conversations and international exchange, some is better than none at all.

Flavor and Essence / Culture and Subculture

Our geopolitical survival may depend on our making an effort with unfamiliar or elusive international things. And, after the difficulty we have already acknowledged, the process may turn out to be easier than we had thought. There are two reasons for this, or two ideas that we might keep in mind. In other lands there will be assumptions that we don't share, or systems we don't understand. But there are also things that we do know, and that we have in common. Their food may have exotic seasonings and unfamiliar flavors, but their food, like ours, is made up of grains and vegetables and proteins. And like us, they eat it together. They may be driving on the wrong—which is to say the other—side of the road, but they are still driving to work, or to play, or to their homes. The flavor, or the method, may be foreign. Many of the essentials end up being familiar.

Another thing helps us as initial cross-cultural difficulties give way to greater comprehension. It relates to what we were just saying about quarterbacks and country music. The fact is that there are also things right here at home that we don't quite get, or like. That which challenges us in the foreign place has parallels in our

31

own backgrounds. But the thing we like, or the thing that we don't, doesn't exhaust the possibilities or complete the picture. No place is simply all this, or all that. Homogeneity may be apparent, or partial, but heterogeneity is the final reality. To put it another way, however plain that place may seem, it will have unsuspected complexities. Every culture is inflected or contradicted by sub-cultures, and every current has its counter.

We have seen that history works similarly. It rewards our study because we learn things we didn't know, or increase our capacities by coming to understand and maybe incorporate something unfamiliar or challenging. Simultaneously, history arouses latent affinities with things that were previously unfamiliar, or shows us a new side of things with which we were already sympathetic. Our lives are enriched as a result. All this applies just as much to the international; the strange and the familiar are brought together, requiring us to work, and rewarding us with increase.

Tourism

How then, can we effectively and successfully approach another country, or another culture? There are a number of methods, and a few pitfalls of which we should be aware. Here is one of the latter. Some of us, sometimes, generalize. We try to find simple, or single causes for the phenomena around us. Generalizations are reassuring, and they can be partly true. They can also be sort of superficial, or our understanding of the generalized thing can be superficial. In our cultural interactions, the results can be unfortunate, and maybe serious.

There is beer in Germany and there are berets and accordions in France. Scottish men do sometimes wear kilts, and they may be seen eating shortbread as they do so. Canadians, or at least many millions of them, really do love hockey. But if we are not careful, some of these emblems, some of the easy symbols of national culture, can end up becoming cultural clichés and stereotypes. Severed from their roots and removed from their context (cf. our discussion on nostalgia), they can cease to signify. They remain only to dazzle the distracted tourist, or endanger the unwary native.

Tourism is not necessarily to blame. Most of us have a desire to travel, to see and enjoy distant places, to learn about and appreciate different customs. Most of us have means that are at least somewhat limited, and so we can only fill this desire very occasionally, and glancingly. We do so by briefly becoming tourists. In real life there is nothing at all wrong with this. For all the limitations, or partialities of touring, its benefits and pleasures are very great.

But beyond literal, practical travel, there are implications. What comes to mind when you think of a tourist? Cameras and clicking and sightseeing tours provide part of the picture. Tourists can be found on the Grand Canal in Venice, crossing San Francisco's Bay Bridge, at the Eiffel tower in Paris or the opera house in Sydney or London's Buckingham Palace. Fair enough. They also look for Anne Shirley on Prince Edward Island, of for hobbits in New Zealand, or for something Harry Potterlike across the United Kingdom. They can sort of miss the point of a place. And while they impose, or judge the far away thing on their own domestic terms, tourists can occasionally be condescending, or impatient, or they engage in compare and contrast exercises that can often end in the impatient dismissal of some inexplicable native custom, or some inexplicable native.

Residency, and the Native Informant

How can we avoid these problems and pitfalls? Tourism has its satisfactions, but there is a more excellent way. A country's celebrated high points are a representation and an expression of precious, central things. The Louvre, or the *Musée d'Orsay*, attracts those crowds for very good reason. But the high points do not represent the whole reality. Substantial touring can bring you into contact with a nation's emblems. Residing gives you its essence.

We benefit greatly and learn profoundly when we do more than just visit a place. Ethnography is the study of culture. When ethnographers go to study a culture that is not native to them, they do a couple of important things. One is that they get close, and they stay on. Unlike the tourist, the ethnographer seeks and embraces the everyday. He is interested in the routines of residency, in the processes and durations of both leisure and labor. In this his work obviously resembles that of the documentarian. Tourism can be like an escapist film: fun, fine, and not quite representative. Residency is longer, harder, and better. Ethnographers, and foreign film fans, come to know this.

When we watch lots of international films we basically start to pile up residency hours. This is especially true with the art films aforementioned, as well as with casual commercial productions. From both of these poles we start to notice certain intonations and gestures, certain systems or cultural solutions. We get a sense of what is typical. At the same time, we start to notice those subcultures and countercurrents we have already considered. Instead of idealizing homogeneity, or xenophobic bigotry, we get complexity, and start to approach completeness.

Ethnographers and any other sensitive visitors really have to be humble. A trained and knowledgeable ethnographer is still an outsider. To bridge the gap she enlists the aid of what is called a native informant. A native informant resides in and belongs to a place. He or she may be somewhat blinded by his or her subjectivity, or to the substance of local things that he or she takes for granted. But as the native informant provides his or her insider's view, the ethnographer starts uncovering roots and rhythms. She starts to belong, and to understand.

For non-ethnographers, for the open-minded and open-hearted person who feels herself to be a citizen of her community, her country, and of the earth, international cinema is an authoritative, necessary native informant. We can't usually travel to very many places. Arranging residency is even more difficult or prohibitive than touring. Since these things are true, we actually need foreign literature and media. We need them as we seek peaceful international relations, even if that peace will only ever be tenuous and partial. We need international voices to guide and warn and bolster us, as we attempt to solve our problems, or accomplish any kind of mutual comprehension. More, we need them if we are going to actually see and enjoy and love one another. When we seek them, as well as an appreciation of our own native realities, some of that vision, and some of those abiding relations, will be ours.

CHAPTER 5
THE ELEMENTS

Story

Linear Narrative

We've spoken of good and bad, fiction and fact, and of historical and international voices. These are all well and good, all fairly incontrovertible, and all too general. How do we actually make contact, with movies and then, with the deeper insights they've given us, with the world itself? The best way is surely to get out and live, to learn and try and experience things. That is not simply to say that we scurry around. If we were to return to the idea of developing critical thinking skills, or assuming a scholar's mindset, then we would have to add a great deal of reflection to our scurrying.

This reflection need not bust the brain, or be separate from familiar, pleasurable pursuit. In Plato's *Apology* we find Socrates proclaiming that the unexamined life is not worth living. Though there are many who dismiss its place (Plato himself had severe doubts about the theatre), it is the position of this book that story is an essential supplement to our existing and experiencing. Stories, in their many forms, give focus to the examination that we make of our lives. They function as parables to teach the thoughtful reader—and viewer—about how, or how not to live.

Narrative means that someone made up this story, which may be true, or less so, and that you to whom it's being narrated, had best pay attention. *Linear*? A common, familiar form through which story is, and for a long time has been, imparted. Here are some of the elements.

Linearity

This section and the next contain the key elements of what is, or at least what is generally considered to be, the classic way to tell a story. What does "classic" mean? Several definitions might do: something with an ideal structure, something that perfectly combines form and content, something that is useful, accessible *and* substantial, something that has stood the test of time. "Classic" also refers to the classical period, to Greece and Rome. Most of what follows is said to come from Aristotle, to whom we've already referred. Aristotle was a Greek philosopher and scientist from the 4th century BC, a time that in many ways represents the height of classical civilization. It's true that Aristotle did say some of this story stuff, sort of. Some of it is reasonably derived from his sometimes sketchy statements (see *Poetics* especially). Anyway—the rules are pretty simple.

Linear narratives start at the beginning, are followed by a middle, and end with an end. In that order. It is generally true in this tradition that anything that might distract from the central narrative, from the mandate to move the story forward at all costs, is considered to be superfluous, and is eliminated. Flashbacks, idyllic or lyrical interludes, plot multiplications—all might qualify in this context as superfluities. This means that at it best a linear narrative is clear and efficient and effective in its entertaining and, sometimes, teaching. It could also mean that at its cynically commercial worst, linear narratives aren't known for stopping and smelling any roses, or for stopping for the casualties at the side of the road.

Dramatic Structure

Watch here for the italicized terms. They are very familiar, they are important, and they work. At the center of the classical linear narrative there is a protagonist. This does not mean that she is necessarily the good guy; she is simply the person around whom the story's main action revolves. The protagonist seeks an objective. Adding a protagonist to an objective, or at least the seeking thereof, might be said to constitute plot. From that seeking we usually get the specific structure of a linear narrative. The protagonist always encounters obstacles to the accomplishment of her objective. If the obstacle is a character, he or she is called the antagonist (who is not always a bad guy).

At the beginning of a linear story there is usually balance. Something happens to cause an imbalance, and the rest of the story is spent trying to restore the original equilibrium. The moment of disequilibrium is called the inciting incident. As the protagonist pursues his or her objective we experience what is called rising action. (By the way, it is possible to have multiple objectives and contradictory obstacles, which is where simple plots become complex, and where we might edge all the way into non-linearity.) The crisis is the moment of the story's highest tension, where we don't know what will happen. Remember that this happening should relate to the original objective. The climax is what happens when the tension is resolved, things are decided, the objective obtained or not. Tying up of loose ends is called the denouement, or falling off. All this holds in every medium, and possible variations within the standard structure are practically infinite. No wonder it's classical.

Story: Non-Linear Narrative

Conventional linear storytelling, as time honored and effective as it may be, is over-represented on our bed tables and in our movie rental receipts. The same old ways can say the same old things—boy gets girl, boy gets fortune, boy blows up stuff, girl sits around rolling her eyes—and they can get plain boring. On the other hand alternative approaches can open up new possibilities. Non-linear narratives can make it more challenging for the viewer or reader, or more interesting. We can rise to the challenge and enjoy a fresh take on things.

There are many effective alternatives to the linear norm. Instead of the pro-pulsion of protagonists reaching for objectives, some stories meander, or slow down, or indulge in pleasurable digressions. Non-linear approaches sometimes make the storytelling, or even the medium itself, the subject of inquiry. This helps us constructively question the thing being presented, and perhaps to advantageously apply some of what we consider to our own circumstances.

A story can dispense with straight chronology, flashing back and forward, in and out to suggest subjectivity, multiplicity, or that the connections between cause and effect are not as direct and inevitable as we might think. Finally, some less linear tales remind us that motivations aren't always clear, endings aren't always happy, and that we're heir to difficulties that test our mettle and demand our compassion for others.

Story: A Range of Possibilities

In Chapter 1, we discussed the advantages of judging a thing on its own terms. This idea is especially important if we want to understand and appreciate stories, and the rich range of narrative strategies that can make them so challenging and rewarding.

There are many ways to tell a tale. There are as many ways to read one. In other words, instead of imposing our preconceptions on a story, we should take the time to identify the ideas that inform it. Just as importantly—form and content can't be separated—we should try to identify the techniques and structures that correspond with a story's ideas. If we're going to judge, or even better, if we're going to analyze and understand and internalize, then we need to be aware of the rules that are operating.

Tragedy and Realism

Here are a few examples among many. Classical tragedies portray the fall of their protagonist. They describe the interactions of fate and human error that ultimately prevail over their characters, however intelligent or virtuous or powerful they may be. As can be imagined, tragedies do not have happy endings, at least on the face of them. There is a paradox built in to the tragedy, however, that keeps it from being merely negative, or nihilistic. In great falls there emerges great nobility. In difficulty, both experienced and witnessed, there is instruction and improvement.

In addition to Greek or Elizabethan notions of what tragedy should properly be, we have more recently come to understand that a character does not have to be a monarch for his fall to have tragic magnitude, or nobility. The loss of the least has ramifications for the sensitively attuned.

This last idea also relates to realism, or some of the forms of realism. Many realist stories are activist in nature, enumerating crises and their causes, things that affect regular people, and regular people who are oppressed or disadvantaged. These stories will often feature exposés of perceived wrong, or activist calls for reform. They will often have an implied or even explicit bias.

To reiterate, some evaluative criticism, especially that rooted in the opinions of the evaluator, may be quick to dismiss or condemn this kind of material, especially if it contradicts the writer's own preferences and assumptions. The spirit of this present publication suggests that we should do otherwise. We give the story the room, and the courtesy, to accomplish the task it has set for itself. If that task is not immoral or dangerous, then we allow it to work within us, to unsettle and expand us. If we judge, we at least partly do so on the story's own terms.

Instead of happy or tragic endings, a realistic narrative will often end ambiguously. Or, to return to a concept discussed earlier, it will reflect aperture instead of closure. Most of our life events have components that are both positive and negative, and most of our so-called stories don't really end very neatly. Alternatively, another kind of realist narrative will concentrate on the typical. It will often feature regular people, speaking in the vernacular, doing regular things.

With regard to film, the realist style, as identified by André Bazin and practiced, for instance, by Jean Renoir, features long camera takes and action played out across many planes of action (the foreground, the midground, the background). Everything is related, and complicatedly. In this kind of film the clear motivations and conclusions of classical/commercial Hollywood are replaced by a daunting and uplifting multiplicity. The meaning and significance of it all is not necessarily clear, or it is so abundant that each reader/viewer will carry away a different set of feelings and insights.

Abundance

Are you getting the idea? There are many approaches to story, each at least somewhat specific, or exclusive in its aims and means. We do well to familiarize ourselves with them. A farce is chock-full of incident, often of a coincidental or implausible nature. This implausibility is not a flaw, as it might be in a psychological narrative. It is part of the stylization, the musicalness, the joy of the form.

A satire may also strain our ideas of likelihood. It exaggerates and subverts in order to disrupt, to make a point, or to suggest an alternative. Naturalism is related to realism, except that it dispenses with calls to action, or any explicit moral judgment at all. It is characterized by a thorough, even an obsessive rendering of milieu, connected with its concern for the influence of environment, and heredity, on people. Naturalism may be very harsh, often concentrating on unseemly actions and distressing subjects. In its unflinching way it says that these things, too, are true. Naturalism may also, if we allow it, present us with evidence, with the raw material with which we can enact our own activism or social intervention.

There is more. Absurdist stories eschew the active, autonomous protagonists of conventional narratives. Objectives are often meaningless, or preposterous. Instead of character arc or increase, these stories often portray a frustrating inertia. Again, this is a stylized form, and resemblance to reality, beyond a number of profound figurative parallels, is not being sought. Much comedy operates in an absurdist register, as well as many searing, poignant expressions of sorrow and despair.

38

Expressionism concerns itself with the search for transcendence (God, truth, happiness, etc.) in another figurative, stylized landscape. This one is transformed by technology, the effects of which are often portrayed as being destructive. Expressionist endings also tend not to be happy, and unlike straight tragedy, there may not be much nobility or instruction in them. We may not like stories like this, but inasmuch as they express the fears and experiences of many of our fellow creatures, and inasmuch as they treat of issues and conditions that can or will affect us all, it behooves us to attend to them anyway.

We might continue, since there are many more story templates than those mentioned, and than we may have suspected. There are yarns and page-turners, didactic narratives, psychological stories, epic tales and explicitly ideological or political ones. There are existential statements, and numerous forms of fragmentation. There are any number of stories that reach for and even touch upon the transcendent. Each of these approaches have distinct characteristics, and those artists making use of them draw upon a range of particular devices relating to each one. Readers and viewers do well when they familiarize themselves with each one. All of these approaches are only a part of a bigger narrative and social picture. They have limitations, or perhaps delimitations. They are also, every one of them, important and valid and true.

For now, and for our purposes, this much is sufficient. There is only to add that, for all our discussions about avoiding hasty judgment and being open to unfamiliar forms, it is still true, and proper, that we will prefer or gravitate toward only some of the stories referred to above. In the end we like certain ideas, and certain forms of expressing them. Far from being inappropriate, these natural predilections are part of what make us as individuals and communities.

The aim of these conversations is to help us enjoy these preferred or privileged statements more substantially, and therefore more abundantly. Linked with this objective is the idea that we must occasionally, even frequently take the time to consider things that are not native to us, or that reflect unfamiliar and possibly uncomfortable perspectives. Each kind of story is important, and valid, and true. As we try to balance bravery and prudence, as we expose ourselves to a wide range of stories and ideas, our narrative vocabularies expand, as well as our social power and usefulness. More simply, we will find meaning and pleasure in more ways, and in more things than we have done before.

Film Crafts

This conversation has been concerned primarily with concepts. We have been talking about ideas, and we have considered a good number of them, from a number of angles. Now, as we come to a close, we will touch upon some practical matters. Conceptual flights, however exhilarating, need grounding, and testing. Here are some brief, practical perspectives on filmmaking, and on the crafts that constitute it.

Direction

The director has the most envied and romanticized job in film production. It's also the hardest job to pin down. What exactly does a film director do? As it turns out, there are many styles and approaches to direction, which vary according to each individual. More than that, the direction of that individual changes with each situation in which he or she finds himself or herself. Who's putting up the money? Who's the client? What's the market? Who are the collaborators, and how many?

These are not especially romantic considerations, and the reality is that there's lots of plain business to take care of before the fabled art of direction comes into play (if it ever does). Anyway, regardless of the configuration, the production details, even the skill of the individual, three things should always be in operation when we think of direction in film or media. First, the director organizes, visualizes, makes flesh a script, a concept, some sort of scenario that probably predates his or her involvement. Second, the director directs, or supervises the activities of his or her production collaborators. And finally, the director directs and draws the attention of the viewer in order to evoke some reaction or emotion.

Acting

Our interest in movies and in the film industry in general often begins with movie stars. We admire their poise and beauty, envy the apparent ease and glamour of their lives, and are willing to pay over and over again to be in their company, if only by proxy and at a distance. Of course this is not a universal state of affairs, but it was the ideal toward which the old Hollywood studios and their relentless publicity machines worked. The star was the industry's main and most marketable commodity, and to a substantial degree, the star still is. This can obviously mean that actors are emblematic of the bill of goods that producers—who, increasingly, are the actors themselves—often try to sell us. But since commodities can sometimes be pleasing, even useful and life-improving, we should be open to and occasionally grateful for the pleasure that these stars can bring us.

This is especially true when we remember that there is a lot more to this picture than just the headliners and their Oscar bids. The fact is that acting is an ancient and even honorable craft that can, in its multitudes of valid styles and approaches, teach us things about ourselves that we need to know. One of these things is that really we're all actors; we pitch and present ourselves and play roles every day. This may not always be to our benefit, but by concentrating on and learning about the subject of acting the casual withholdings and deceptions of our everyday interactions can actually be turned to comprehension and compassion.

Our objectives, tactics

Design

The spatial or environmental arts—architecture, interior design, carpentry and costume design and landscaping and on and on—are arguably more important, and are certainly more immediate than the representational and narrative arts that seem most often catch our attention. These things provide the settings and fittings for our lives, and they most powerfully inflect the experiences we have as we live. When we become sensitive to our surroundings, the power to understand and enjoy and even change through attending to these surroundings increases.

If production design in films is traditionally subordinate to story and enactment, it is still essential to our deepened experiences with story. In addition it might be observed that where stories and directorial concepts and such very often fall seriously short, design in films tends to be consistently excellent. Here is where we can learn an important arts lesson that extends much further than our present discussion: there's almost always something substantially good in a film, if we'll learn and then look for it. When our feelings are mixed and our experiences not all they could be, there is still much of benefit that we can derive, if we'll only concentrate.

Cinematography

The word "movie" and the phrase "motion picture" remind us that, for all our story preoccupations, the image is arguably the key to and the centre of the medium. The old filmmakers' maxim, coined in part to distance films from the parent arts of stage and page, was "don't say it—show it." The movies' uniqueness and appeal lie partly in the way that they communicate visually. This communication is not necessarily just conceptual, or story-related. Pictures, composed and lit and moving on the screen, can bypass the analytical and go straight tot the heart of the matter. For good or ill, our strongest, most stirring movie memories are probably visual.

This is also a point that many critics of the media would make; pornographic or exploitatively violent images work through the visual. These critics certainly have their points, but there is more to say. Are pictures dangerous? Well, maybe, but not only. As always, a little knowledge and discussion can help us over potential rough spots. Then, after learning and discussing, we'll find that rough spots are just a small part of the abundant reality. Movies provide a practically endless supply of ravishing, rapturous images, leading to practically endless instructions and delights.

Editing

So, one school of thought has it that the image is the unique key to movies, and to movie enjoyment. As is usually the case, this good argument can be countered by another, just as convincing. In the early 1920s a group of Soviet theorist/filmmakers came up with the theory of *montage*, which is basically that editing is the foundation of cinematic art, and that meaning in movies is not found within single images, but rather that it is created in the juxtaposition of those images, and of the concepts affixed to them. One might dispute some of the Soviets' specific formulations, but it is hard to deny that it is largely through editing that film stories are told and film ideas are communicated.

It is also true that a powerful juxtaposition can be as visceral and transporting—and maybe as dangerous—as a powerful image. Advertisers and propagandists work their persuasions and deceptions through montage. We need to remember that their juxtapositions—of consumer and product and purchase, of idea and its inevitability—are not necessarily as desirable and as natural as they would have us believe. We need to remember that it's not just the people we disagree with that manipulate as they seek to persuade. We also need to remember that all this juxtaposing is not inherently or necessarily as sinister as we might suppose. Individuality, community, history: all are made as we assemble masses of fact and perception, choice and action. Not only films, but even our lives can be seen as montage constructions, assemblies made from the conscious combining of the pieces at hand.

Music and Sound

Silent movies were almost never silent. They were accompanied by pianists or organists, small ensembles or large orchestras, all of which added to the presentational, stylized nature of that period's cinema experience. When sound came in the late 1920s and early 1930s (depending on where you lived), a lot of that bracing, open artificiality disappeared. The presentational gave way to a sort of—this was Hollywood—realism. That meant that for the most part sound had to be practically motivated, and that music was relegated to a very paradoxical and powerful back seat.

This is the place of classical film music, the functions of which largely prevail to this day. The idea is that film music acts as a handmaid, supportive of and subservient to narrative, an enhancer of the story's effects, an almost subliminal influence on the spectator, whom it leads gently but firmly in the way he should go. Sound good? Can be—many wonderful classical scores have added nuance and poignancy to already powerful films, to everyone's satisfaction. But this classical music has sometimes had a smothering effect as well, it has been used to paper over gaps and disguise shabby stretches of inadequate films, and it can keep the viewer from the sometimes ambiguity and often rich multiplicity of film narrative. There are alternatives to classical Hollywood function, in both sound and music, which do two things. They spice things up, and in so spicing, take the burden of exclusivity—this is the only course—from the classical, and help it work the way it should, as part of a range of valid and pleasing possibilities.

Filmmaking

We have just been isolating the elements of film to try to see what they are and how they operate. We need to remember though that in real life it's all part of a package; film is a definitively collaborative art, and it is from the combination and interaction of elements that its meaning and pleasure, positive and negative, derives. Not incidentally, awareness of these combinations also suggests the next steps in a film student's education. Difference in approach or circumstance leads to different kinds of filmmaking and film understanding. As we become sensitive to the contributions that the various film crafts make to the ensemble, we are ready for some bigger pictures, ready to consider and enjoy different styles, genres, idioms, periods, national cinemas. As we're introduced to all these ways to make films, we're reminded, just as importantly, that there are lots of ways to take films. This has been maintained through the course of this book: reading film is at least as important as producing it. When through effort and experience we become media literate, when we've read enough to recognize and value different options and alternatives, then we approach the end of narcissistic, self-absorbed viewing. We approach the point where we can turn every appropriate media choice to our own enjoyment and advantage.

CHAPTER 6
WRITING A REVIEW

Now for one last thing. This book has been a long conversation about critical thinking and media literacy. As implied by this last section about film crafts, there remains to apply its concepts in some practical setting, or to some practical task. For college student and non-matriculated observer alike, here are a few ideas that can help you gather your thoughts and impressions into concrete and coherent expression.

Gathering Information

Now it's time to think about writing a paper, or a review. Film artists almost always have to balance the things that they want to say with the expectations or requirements of sponsors or patrons. Film students have to do the same. Such constraints are often looked upon negatively. They needn't be, at least not always. Restrictions and requirements can help us to focus, to discipline ourselves, to direct and give pleasing, useful shape to our previously unorganized impressions.

As you prepare to write your paper you will be doing a number of things, many of them similar to those we have been considering throughout this book. You will want to establish the exact nature of your assignment. What is being asked of you? Is there a particular form or style that you will be expected to use? If the assignment is more open-ended, is there a form or style that you can identify, a particular approach that will be most effective in helping you to shape your thoughts?

Film Reviews

If you are writing a film review, then you will want to prepare by reading a fairly wide range of critical material, and a wide range of critics. You want to familiarize yourself with some of the conventions and expectations of the form. You may also want to familiarize yourself with some of the alternatives to convention, with reviewers or periodicals that go against the grain of things.

Some of your critical reading may relate to the specific film at hand, though you will want to guard against being overly swayed, positively or negatively, by what the professionals are saying. It is also a good idea, if you have the time, to familiarize yourself with other related films. What else has this director directed, or this writer written? What kind of things has this studio or film organization been putting out? What does the competing or contemporary product look like?

Now comes the time to do your own work. Ideally—and if you plan, instead of procrastinating, the ideal should always be attainable—you will watch the film a number of times. (This option does not normally exist for a professional reviewer, and some professional reviewers—Pauline Kael made this an article of faith—would reject the option if they had it. Most of you are not professional reviewers. See the film a number of times.) The first time through is for fun, for impressions of story and the way the story is communicated, for the general feelings the film gives you.

After this first viewing, while your thoughts are fresh, jot down some general notes. A subsequent glance through these notes should give you some hints about what to look for, or what to concentrate on, the next time around. On your second pass you might think about theme, or style, or the ways in which each relates to the other. In addition you might think about some of the parallels between this film and the culture from which it came, or in which you find yourself. A further, probably final run through will help you identify the scenes you will use to illustrate your points, or the elements—lighting, or silence, or color, or the lack of it—utilized by the filmmakers to make theirs.

History and Theory

We are drawn to films, and to filmmakers, because of their creativity. We are inspired by the skill and imagination, the meaning and substance of what we find in the cinema. When writing about or responding to movies it is natural to want to do so as creatively as possible.

Students undertaking scholarly work need to resist that urge, at least if we are thinking of creativity as it is conventionally defined. A scholarly paper is neither an improvisation nor an editorial. It should be carefully and clearly structured, carefully and clearly—and, we might say, modestly—written. That is to say that the style or wit of the writer is less important than the object of inquiry. The scholar's duty is to her material, and her allegiance to the field of knowledge.

So, whether you are just starting out or you have some publications under your belt, there are certain things that are expected of you. You will likely watch a film or group of films. You will also consult a wide range of critical material: reviews, periodicals and books. You may have occasion to consult with archivists and visit their archives. You will need to interpret, prioritize and synthesize the findings of previous scholars. At the same time you will need to gather your own thoughts. You will need to shape and form and work toward your own hypotheses.

Sometimes you will see something called a "works cited" list. These lists contain fewer items than a bibliography, which means that scholars consult more works than they actually draw upon or quote from in their published work. This is a solemn and unavoidable fact. Scholars have a great deal to read and do. As you write your scholarly paper you should start broadly, and then start winnowing and focusing. In order to successfully do that, you will want to consult a number of print and online directories, as well as a reference librarian. You are looking for what is called an abstract, which is a brief description of a paper's subject and conclusions. An abstract will tell a writer whether the abstracted work relates to her research. Similarly the forwards and introductions of scholarly books can tell us whether or how we need the material within them.

This may all sound a bit daunting, especially if you are in an introduction to film class. Relax. Peer reviewed publication is not likely, and is almost certainly not expected of you. If you are afraid of the library or, more appropriately, if you are not expected to do all of the work just described, a number of simpler courses are open to you. Your introduction and history classes will be using one of any number of film textbooks. All of these will have general bibliographies, a selected list of titles that relate to particular subjects, and that will start to point you in the right direction. Having first made your own preliminary list of relevant works—professors don't help students that haven't first made their own inquiries—you may also want to consult with your instructor. He or she will help you compile a short list of titles that are relevant to your topic.

The result of all this work won't be complete, or comprehensive. It might not even be very good, at least the first few times. Don't worry, and especially, don't quit. Film writing is as big and challenging as learning to play that musical instrument. It takes practice to get the knack.

Tone

Reviews tend to be more casual, more conversational than scholarly work. Even so, it is usually true that a certain formality attends most critical writing. We should acknowledge something here: in most of the papers that you might write, especially in a scholarly register, the tone of the present publication would not be appropriate. Its direct address, the "you" and the "we," the contractions and vernacular expressions would not pass muster with most editors, or their publications.

This is not an apology; we hope and believe that the tone of the present conversation, as one being held between sympathetic people embarking on a challenging and enjoyable field of study, is appropriate. But be aware. Publications and editors dictate the kind of tone and the nature of writing that they want. As you learn about this field, as you establish the kinds of things you want to say and the way you want to say them, you will still be substantially and even advantageously subject to the dictates of journalistic and scholarly convention.

Your Turn...

There are too many valid ways to write about film for us to address them all here. Some of the options are referred to in this book's appendices. You might also ask your teachers for examples of what they feel to be successful reviews or scholarly papers. Ask them to identify the specific effective components of these writings. Then read for yourself, and see what you think. Remembering the validity of convention and the importance of humility, start to identify the things that you find important, and the ways you might like to work and express yourself within established scholarly parameters. Then, now, proceed...

APPENDIX A
FILMOGRAPHY

Lists like this are always arbitrary. They are gap-filled by nature, frequently eccentric and sometimes plain indefensible. We might venture to say that our cultural habit of list-making is at its core pretty suspect; where the intent is not to hoodwink people in order to close their minds and/or steal their money, then at the very least our top-ten tendencies reduce our awareness of complex reality and close conversations that should just be beginning. Therefore—here's another list, containing a ton of really cool titles that are worth investigating. There are too many movies here, so that you'll remember that the tip is just a small part of the iceberg, that isolating what's "best" isn't as important or as fun as identifying what's good, and so you'll have a few years' worth of hints about where to go with your new cinematic interests.

All this suggests, by the way, something that is awfully important to remember as we watch films. Although it might be argued that there are some plain perfect productions in the lists below, it's also true that several of these films are flawed, messy, in conflict with themselves: in other words they are human documents that may require, and then reward your patience and consideration. It also goes without saying that you should inform yourself before watching; some viewers may deem some of this material to be inappropriate. The films are listed by topic, and they all have some substantial relationship to or bearing upon that topic. Notice too that most to all of these films could just as well be listed under any number of the other categories. It's good to isolate elements, but in the end film is a thoroughly collaborative and integrative art. Happy reading!

Standards

The Apartment (1960)
The Best Man (1964)
Black Beauty (1994)
Breaker Morant (1979)
Christmas in July (1940)
Common Threads: Stories from the
    Quilt (1989)
Crossfire (1947)
The Crucible (1997)
Day of Wrath (1943)
Dead Man Walking (1995)
Dekalog V: Thou Shalt Not Kill
    (1989)
The Defiant Ones (1958)

La Dolce Vita (1960)
Enchanted April (1991)
A Face in the Crowd (1957)
Gandhi (1982)
Glory (1989)
Groundhog Day (1992)
I Am a Fugitive from a Chain Gang
    (1932)
Intruder in the Dust (1949)
The Killing Fields (1984)
Lorenzo's Oil (1992)
Madame Bovary (1991)
A Man for All Seasons (1966)
Matewan (1987)

My Night at Maud's (1969)
Nazarin (1958)
The Nightmare Before Christmas
  (1993)
Ordinary People (1980)
The Ox-bow Incident (1943)

Room at the Top (1959)
Searching for Bobby Fischer (1993)
To Kill a Mockingbird (1962)
Twelve Angry Men (1957)
Z (1968)

History

The Big Parade (1925)
By the Law (1926)
Cabiria (1914)
Chang (1927)
The Cheat (1915)
The Crowd (1928)
The General (1926)
Greed (1924)
He Who Gets Slapped (1924)
The Iron Horse (1924)
The Kid (1921)
The Kid Brother (1927)
The Last Command (1928)
The Last Laugh (1924)
The Mark of Zorro (1920)
The Marriage Circle (1924)

Mutual Comedies (1917-18)
My Best Girl (1927)
Napoleon (1927)
Orphans of the Storm (1921)
The Passion of Joan of Arc (1928)
Regeneration (1915)
Seventh Heaven (1927)
The Sons of Ingmar/Karin
  Ingmarsdotter (1919-20)
Spies (1928)
Stella Dallas (1926)
The Ten Commandments (1923)
Tol'able David (1921)
Les Vampires (1915)
Wings (1927)

Documentary

35 Up (1991)
American Dream (1990)
Anne Frank Remembered (1995)
The Battle of Chile (1973-78)
The Beatles Anthology (1995)
Chronicle of a Summer (1961)
Close-Up (1990)
Dead Birds (1963)
A Diary for Timothy (1945)
Drifters (1929)
Four Little Girls (1997)
Gates of Heaven (1978)
Hoop Dreams (1994)
Hospital (1970)
It's All True (1993)

Kanehsatake... (1990)
The Last Waltz (1978)
Manufacturing Consent... (1992)
Nanook of the North (1922)
Pumping Iron (1976)
The Rise to Power of Louis XIV
  (1966)
Sans Soleil (1983)
Shoah (1986)
The Silent World (1956)
The Sorrow and the Pity (1970)
The Thin Blue Line (1988)
The Times of Harvey Milk (1984)
Turksib (1929)
Unknown Chaplin (1982)

War Game (1965)

International

The 400 Blows (1959)
Aguirre, the Wrath of God (1972)
Au Revoir Les Enfants (1987)
The Ballad of Gregorio Cortez (1982)
The Battle of Algiers (1965)
Beauty and the Beast (1946)
Bicycle Thieves (1948)
Black Rain (1989)
Black Orpheus (1959)
The Blue Kite (1993)
La Ciudad (1998)
Cleo from 5 to 7 (1962)
The Fireman's Ball (1967)
Fires on the Plain (1959)
The Grand Illusion (1939)
Harakiri (1962)

Killer of Sheep (1977)
Man of Iron (1981)
My Brilliant Career (1979)
Los Olvidados (1948)
Pather Panchali (1955)
Pelle the Conqueror (1988)
The Professionals (1966)
Rome Open City (1945)
Sanjuro (1962)
The Story of Qiu Ju (1992)
Strangers in Good Company/The
    Company of Strangers (1990)
Strictly Ballroom (1992)
The White Balloon (1995)
Wild Strawberries (1957)

Linear Narrative

Ace in the Hole (1951)
Adam's Rib (1949)
All About Eve (1950)
Angels with Dirty Faces (1938)
Babe (1995)
Bad Day at Black Rock (1954)
Bachelor Mother (1939)
Bombshell (1933)
Casablanca (1942)
Dead End (1937)
Dr. Ehrlich's Magic Bullet (1940)
Force of Evil (1948)
The Freshman (1925)
The Glass Menagerie (1987)
Great Expectations (1946)
The Iron Giant (1999)
It Happened One Night (1934)

Jean de Florette/Manon des Sources
    (1986)
The Lady Eve (1941)
The Man Who Shot Liberty Valance
    (1962)
Of Mice and Men (1939)
One Hundred Men and a Girl (1937)
Places in the Heart (1984)
The Philadelphia Story (1940)
A Star is Born (1937)
Shoeshine (1946)
Steamboat Bill Jr. (1927)
Sweet Smell of Success (1957)
Toy Story (1995)
The Trial (1961)
Young Mr. Lincoln (1939)

Non-Linear Narrative

The American Friend (1977)
American Graffiti (1973)
Blockheads (1938)
The Conversation (1974)
The Dead (1987)
Dead of Night (1945)
Dr. Strangelove... (1964)
Duck Soup (1933)
Endless Summer (1964)
Eyes Without a Face (1959)
A Hard Day's Night (1964)
The Incredible Shrinking Man (1957)
The Killing (1956)
The Last Days (1999)
On Approval (1943)
Playtime (1967)

Rashomon (1950)
Roger and Me (1989)
Secrets and Lies (1995)
Sherlock Junior (1924)
The Southerner (1946)
The Spanish Prisoner (1997)
The Story of GI Joe (1945)
The Straight Story (1999)
The Third Man (1948)
Thirty Two Short Films About Glenn
    Gould (1993)
The Vanishing (1988)
Waiting for Fidel (1974)
A Walk in the Sun (1945)
Where is the Friend's House? (1989)
Winchester '73 (1950)

Direction

8½ (1963)
Alice in the Cities (1973)
The Asphalt Jungle (1950)
The Awful Truth (1937)
All Quiet on the Western Front
    (1930)
Badlands (1973)
Le Boucher (1969)
Good Morning (1959)
Hail the Conquering Hero (1944)
Hamlet (1948)
I Was a Male War Bride (1948)
King of Kings (1927)
Knife in the Water (1962)
Lady for a Day (1933)
Lawrence of Arabia (1962)
A Man Escaped (1956)

Modern Times (1936)
My Darling Clementine (1946)
Notorious (1946)
Rules of the Game (1939)
Rocco and His Brothers (1960)
The Same Old Song (1997)
Le Samourai (1967)
The Secret of Roan Inish (1995)
The Seventh Seal (1957)
Sunrise (1927)
Tokyo Story (1953)
Touch of Evil (1958)
Ugetsu Monogatari (1953)
Viridiana (1961)
Voyage to Italy (1953)
The Witches (1989)

Acting

Anatomy of a Murder (1959)
Broken Blossoms (1919)
City Lights (1931)

The Color of Paradise (1999)
A Cry in the Dark (1988)
Desert Bloom (1986)

High Sierra (1941)
His Girl Friday (1941)
Hud (1963)
It (1927)
It Started With Eve (1941)
It's a Gift (1934)
The Little Foxes (1941)
Mad Love (1935)
Malcolm X (1992)
Nights of Cabiria (1957)
Ninotchka (1939)
No Man of Her Own (1949)
Not One Less (1999)

The Official Story (1985)
A Passage to India (1985)
Ponette (1996)
Remains of the Day (1993)
Shine (1997)
Sparrows (1926)
A Streetcar Named Desire (1952)
Way Out West (1937)
Wee Willie Winkie (1937)
When We Were Kings (1996)
White Heat (1949)
Will Penny (1968)

Production Design

The Adventures of Baron
    Munchausen (1988)
Babe: A Pig in the City (1998)
Babette's Feast (1987)
The Bride of Frankenstein (1935)
Burden of Dreams (1982)
Dick Tracy (1990)
The Fallen Idol (1948)
Fantastic Voyage (1966)
The Haunting (1963)
Honey, I Shrunk the Kids (1989)
Jane Eyre (1996)
Jeremiah Johnson (1972)
Kanal (1957)
King of the Hill (1993)
Kundun (1997)
A Little Princess (1995)

Metropolis (1926)
Mon Oncle (1958)
The Ox (1991)
Pee Wee's Big Adventure (1985)
Raise the Red Lantern (1991)
Robinson Crusoe on Mars (1964)
A Room with a View (1985)
Scaramouche (1952)
The Scarlet Empress (1934)
Summertime (1955)
The Thief of Baghdad (1924)
The Three Musketeers (1973)
Top Hat (1935)
Tucker: The Man and His Dream
    (1988)
Triumph of the Will (1934)
West Side Story (1961)

Cinematography

The Adventures of Robin Hood
    (1938)
All That Heaven Allows (1955)
Black Narcissus (1947)
The Black Stallion (1979)
Dr. Jekyll and Mr. Hyde (1932)

The Good, the Bad and the Ugly
    (1967)
The Grapes of Wrath (1940)
Heartland (1979)
How Green Was My Valley (1941)
The Last of the Mohicans (1920)

Letter from an Unknown Woman
(1948)
The Magnificent Ambersons (1942)
Microcosmos (1996)
Moana (1926)
Never Cry Wolf (1983)
Out of the Past (1947)
Paths of Glory (1957)
Ride the High Country (1962)
The River (1951)
Salesman (1969)

The Scent of Green Papaya (1993)
The Secret Garden (1993)
Sunday in the Country (1984)
Tabu (1931)
Tokyo Olympiad 1964 (1965)
Visions of Light (1992)
Wait Until Dark (1967)
The Wild Child (1970)
Winter Light (1962)
The Yearling (1946)
Yellow Sky (1948)

Editing

42 Up (1999)
Arachnophobia (1990)
Battleship Potemkin (1925)
Berlin: Symphony of a Great City
(1927)
Buster Keaton: A Hard Act to Follow
(1987)
Cat People (1942)
The End of St. Petersburg (1927)
For All Mankind (1989)
From Russia with Love (1963)
Fury (1936)
Harvest of Shame (1960)
High Noon (1952)
Hotel Terminus (1987)
In the Year of the Pig (1969)
Iron Monkey (1993)
The Indian in the Cupboard (1995)
Intolerance (1916)

Invasion of the Body Snatchers
(1956)
Jaws (1975)
The Legend of the Drunken Master II
(1994)
Mad Max 2 (1981)
The Man with the Movie Camera
(1929)
Mr. Smith Goes to Washington
(1939)
Pickpocket (1959)
Rear Window (1954)
Rocky (1976)
San Francisco (1936)
The Set Up (1948)
The Thing from Another World
(1951)
Whisky Galore! (1949)

Music and Sound

2001: A Space Odyssey (1968)
The Band Wagon (1953)
Brief Encounter (1945)
The Chronicle of Anna Magdalena
Bach (1968)
Crooklyn (1994)
Distant Voices, Still Lives (1988)

The Elephant Man (1980)
Fantasia (1940)
The Gospel According to Matthew
(1964)
The Hunchback of Notre Dame
(1939)
King Kong (1933)

Kings Row (1941)
Laura (1944)
Love Me Tonight (1932)
M (1931)
The Magic Flute (1975)
Le Million (1931)
The Mission (1986)
The Natural (1984)
Night and Fog (1955)
The Plow That Broke the Plains
  (1936)

Pursued (1947)
Raiders of the Lost Ark (1981)
The Sea Hawk (1940)
Singin' in the Rain (1952)
Stop Making Sense (1984)
Swing Time (1936)
Tom Jones (1963)
Toy Story II (1999)
The Umbrellas of Cherbourg (1964)
Vertigo (1958)

Filmmaking

Back to the Future (1985)
Bringing up Baby (1938)
Children of Paradise (1945)
Citizen Kane (1941)
Day for Night (1973)
The Devil and Daniel Webster (1941)
The Emperor and the Assassin (1999)
Gold Diggers of 1933 (1933)
Gone with the Wind (1939)
The Gunfighter (1950)
Henry V (1989)
It's a Wonderful Life (1946)
The Madness of King George (1996)
The Man in the White Suit (1951)
The Manchurian Candidate (1962)
A Matter of Life and Death (1946)

Meet Me in St. Louis (1944)
The Night of the Hunter (1955)
North by Northwest (1959)
Oliver Twist (1948)
On the Waterfront (1954)
Ordet (1955)
Othello (1952)
Raising Arizona (1987)
Ran (1987)
Rio Bravo (1958)
Scaramouche (1923)
The Searchers (1956)
Strawberry Blonde (1942)
To Live (1994)
Treasure of the Sierra Madre (1948)
Went the Day Well? (1942)

APPENDIX B
READINGS AND BIBLIOGRAPHIES

This book has given you an introduction to film, and to some helpful ways of thinking about film. If the book has done its job, and if you have done yours, then you may not be satisfied with a mere introduction. There is much more to learn, and to enjoy. These two part bibliographies are here offered to suggest some next steps. The first part is a selected list of books that relate directly to the topic at hand. The second contains a number of mostly fictional titles that have a strong, if sometimes figurative connection with that topic. (Design-linked texts will strongly evoke environment and setting. Actorly stories will explore the depths and breadths of individuality.)

Standards

Criticism

James Agee, *Agee on Film* (vol. I)
Timothy Corrigan, *A Short Guide to Writing About Film*
Graham Greene (David Parkinson, ed.), *The Graham Greene Film Reader: Reviews, Essays, Interviews and Film Stories*
John Grierson, *Grierson at the Movies*
J. Hoberman, *Vulgar Modernism*
Pauline Kael, *5001 Nights at the Movies*
Peter Lehman, ed., *Close Viewings: An Anthology of New Film Criticism*
C.S. Lewis, *An Experiment in Criticism*
Jonathon Rosenbaum, *Placing Movies*
David Thomson, *A Biographical Dictionary of Film*
Leo Tolstoy, *What Is Art?*
Francois Truffaut, *The Films in My Life*
Wim Wenders, *(E)motion Pictures; The Logic of Images*

Bibliography (Ethics)

Hannah Arendt, *Eichmann in Jerusalem*
Edward Bloor, *Tangerine*
Albert Camus, *The Plague*
George Eliot, *Silas Marner*
James Hogg, *Memoirs and Confessions of a Justified Sinner*
Norton Juster, *The Phantom Tollbooth*
Charles Kingsley, *The Water Babies*
Christopher Marlowe, *Doctor Faustus*
Chaim Potok, *My Name Is Asher Lev*

Anna Sewell, *Black Beauty*
GB Shaw, *Saint Joan*
Mark Twain, *Huckleberry Finn*

History

Bibliography

Robert C. Allen, Douglas Gomery, *Film History, Theory and Practice*
Kevin Brownlow, *The Parade's Gone By*
Noel Burch, *Life to Those Shadows*
Walter Kerr, *The Silent Clowns*
Richard Koszarski, *An Evening's Entertainment: The Age of the Silent Feature Picture, 1915-1928*
Gerald Mast, *A Short History of the Movies; The Movies in Our Midst*
David Robinson, *Chaplin*
Janet Staiger, *Interpreting Films: Studies in the Historical Reception of American Cinema*
Paulo Cherchi Usai, *Burning Passions: An Introduction to the Study of Silent Cinema*
Black Elk, *Black Elk Speaks*
George McKay Brown, *Beside the Ocean of Time*
Confucius, *Analects*
William de Mille, *Hollywood Saga*
Kenneth Grahame, *The Golden Age*
Edith Hamilton, *Mythology*
Seamus Heaney, *Beowulf*

Documentary

Bibliography

Erik Barnouw, *Documentary: A History of the Non-Fiction Film*
Jack Ellis, *The Documentary Idea: A Critical History of the English-Language Documentary Film and Video*
Frances Hubbard Flaherty, *The Odyssey of a Film Maker: Robert Flaherty's Story*
John Grierson, *Grierson on Documentary*
Louis Jacobs, *The Documentary Tradition*
Kevin MacDonald, *Imagining Reality: The Faber Book of Documentary*
Michael Rabiger, *Directing the Documentary*
Leni Riefenstahl, *Memoir*
Alan Rosenthal, *New Challenges for Documentary*
Paul Rotha, *Robert J. Flaherty: A Biography*
William Rothman, *Documentary Film Classics*

International

Bibliography

Roy Armes, *Third World Film Making and the West*
Ingmar Bergman, *Images: My Life in Film*
Luis Buñuel, *My Last Sigh*
Carl-Theodor Dreyer, *Dreyer in Double Reflection*
Jim Hillier, ed., *Cahiers du Cinema* (3 vols.)
Robert Philip Kolker, *The Altering Eye*
Geoffrey Nowell-Smith, *The Oxford History of World Cinema*
Jean Renoir, *Renoir on Renoir*
Judy Stone, *Eye on the World: Conversations with International Filmmakers*
Chinua Achebe, *Things Fall Apart*
Charlotte Bronte, *Jane Eyre*
Bruce Chatwin, *What Am I Doing Here?*
Anton Chekhov, *Forty Stories*
Maxim Gorky, *Childhood*
Graham Greene, *The Power and the Glory*
Herman Hesse, *Siddhartha*
Rudyard Kipling, *Kim*
Jamaica Kincaid, *A Small Place*
Compton Mackenzie, *Whisky Galore*
George Orwell, *Homage to Catalonia*
Satyajit Ray, *Phatik Chand*
Erich Maria Remarque, *All Quiet on the Western Front*
Albert Schweitzer, *On the Edge of the Primeval Forest*
B. Traven, *The Treasure of the Sierra Madre*
Virginia Woolf, *A Room of One's Own*
W.B. Yeats, *Celtic Twilight*

Linear Narrative

Bibliography

Richard Corliss, *The Hollywood Screenwriters*
Syd Field, *Screenplay...*
William Goldman, *Adventures in the Screen Trade: A Personal View of Hollywood Screenwriting*
Ian Hamilton, *Writers in Hollywood*
Pat McGilligan, *Backstory: Interviews...* (3 vols.)
Lillian Ross, *Picture*
Thomas Schatz, *The Genius of the System: Hollywood Filmmaking in the Studio Era*
Lloyd Alexander, *The Book of Three/The Black Cauldron*
Lois Lowry, *Number the Stars*

Katherine Patterson, *The Bridge to Terabithia*
Elizabeth George Speare, *The Witch of Blackbird Pond*

Non-Linear Narrative

Bibliography

Ken Dancyger and Jeff Rush, *Alternative Scriptwriting: Writing Beyond the Rules*
P. Adams Sitney, *Visionary Film: The American Avant-Garde 1943-1978*; *The Avant-Garde Film: A Reader of Theory and Criticism*
Douglas Adams, *The Hitchhiker's Guide to the Galaxy*
Samuel Beckett, *Waiting for Godot*
James M. Cain, *Double Indemnity*
Robert Cormier, *I Am the Cheese*
William Pene Dubois, *The Twenty-One Balloons*
Lewis Carroll, *Through the Looking Glass*
Arthur C. Clarke, *Childhood's End*
Patricia Highsmith, *The Talented Mr. Ripley*
Richard Hughes, *High Wind in Jamaica*
Henry James, *The Turn of the Screw*
Franz Kafka, *The Trial*
Herman Melville, *Moby Dick*
Jim Thompson, *The Killer Inside Me*
Leo Tolstoy, *The Kreutzer Sonata*
Mark Twain, *The Mysterious Stranger*
Elie Wiesel, *Night*

Directing

Bibliography

Peter Bogdanovich, *Who the Devil Made It*
Frank Capra, *The Name Above the Title*
Edward Dmytryk, *On Screen Directing*
Sydney Lumet, *Making Movies*
David Mamet, *On Directing Film*
Michael Powell, *A Life in Movies: An Autobiography*
Andrew Sarris, *The American Cinema*
John Sayles, *Thinking in Pictures: the Making of the Movie* Matewan
Orson Welles (with Peter Bogdanovich), *This Is Orson Welles*

Acting

Bibliography

Michael Caine, *Acting in Film: An Actor's Take on Movie Making*
Richard Dyer, *Stars*
Lillian Gish, *The Movies, Mr. Griffith, and Me*
James Naremore, *Acting in the Cinema*
Konstantin Stanislavski, *An Actor Prepares*
Fyodor Dostoievski, *Notes From the Undergound*
Knut Hamsun, *Hunger*
Kasuo Ishiguro, *Remains of the Day*
Margaret Laurence, *The Stone Angel*
Phillys Reynolds Naylor, *The Agony of Alice*
Leo Tolstoy, *The Death of Ivan Illych*
Anthony Trollope, *The Warden*

Design

Bibliography

Charles Affron and Mirella Jona Affron, *Sets in Motion: Art Direction and Film Narrative*
Léon Barsacq, *Caligari's Cabinet and Other Grand Illusions: A History of Film Design*
Vincent Lobrutto, *By Design: Interviews with Film Production Designers*
Emily Bronte, *Wuthering Heights*
Grey Owl, *Sajo and the Beaver People*
Karen Hesse, *Out of the Dust*
Jack London, *Klondike Tales*
Herman Melville, *Typee*
Frank Norris, *McTeague*
Scott O'Dell, *The Island of the Blue Dolphins*
Gary Paulsen, *Hatchet*
Salman Rushdie, *Haroun and the Sea of Stories*
Alexander Solzhenitsyn, *One Day in the Life of Ivan Denisovich*
Art Spiegelman, *Maus: A Survivor's Tale*
Emile Zola, *Therese Raquin*

Cinematography

Bibliography

André Bazin, *What Is Cinema?* (Vol. I)
Brian Coe, *The History of Movie Photography*

Charles Higham, *Hollywood Cameramen*

Kris Malkiewicz, *Film Lighting: Talks with Hollywood's Cinematographers and Gaffers*

Editing

Bibliography

Ken Dancyger, *The Technique of Film and Video Editing*
Sergei Eisenstein, *Film Form*
Vincent Lo Brutto, *Selected Takes: Film Editors on Film Editing*
Walter Murch, *In the Blink an Eye*
V.I. Pudovkin, *Film Technique*
Karel Reisz, Gavin Millar, *The Technique of Film Editing*
Dziga Vertov, *Kino Eye: The Writings of Dziga Vertov*

Music and Sound

Bibliography

John Belton and Elizabeth Weis, eds., *Film Sound: Theory and Practice*
Leonard Bernstein, *The Unanswered Question*
Royal Brown, *Overtones and Undertones: Reading Film Music*
Michel Chion, *Audio-Vision: Sound on Screen*
Hanns Eisler, *Composing for the Films*
Claudia Gorbman, *Unheard Melodies: Narrative Film Music*
Kathryn Kalinak, *Settling the Score*
Fred Karlin, *Listening to Movies: The Film-Lover's Guide to Film Music*
Clifford McCarty, *Film Music I*
Vincent LoBrutto, *Sound-on-Film: Interviews with Creators of Film Sound*
André Previn, *No Minor Chords*
Tony Thomas, *Film Score: The View from the Podium*

NOTES

NOTES

NOTES

NOTES

NOTES

NOTES

NOTES